Blessings in Elbow Grease

Blessings in Elbow Grease

When All You've Got is Faith and Fight

Ash Davis

For Sue Ellen

*God sure loved you, you chose to love me even though I didn't
deserve it, and I miss you every single day.*

And for Anna

*My editor and friend, thank you a million times over for helping
me make this real. You are a gift.*

Prologue

Perched at a wobbly, second-hand desk in my cramped bedroom, I faced a decision so daunting it stole my breath—I couldn't afford to get this wrong, not with everything on the line. My mind raced, the weight of another life-altering decision in a recent stream of them pressing down on me. The walls of my tiny bedroom seemed to shrink with every passing second. Months ago, Dr. Richard Dew, a trusted mentor, had taught me the power of clarity: write it down, see it laid bare. So, I scrawled out the pros and cons, each word carefully pressing into the page under the gravity of what they represented.

Pro: I'd be fulfilling a lifelong dream.

Pro: It played to my strengths as a marketer.

Pro: It could bring more money into our struggling home.

But then came the cons, each one hitting like a gut punch.

Con: The $1,000 investment was my entire savings, with nothing to catch me if I fell. I'd lost my job months ago without warning and nothing was on the horizon, no matter how many calls I made or applications I filled out.

Con: I had never faced a challenge this daunting. Here I was, where I never thought I'd be, a struggling, out-of-work, single mother dangerously close to negative numbers in her checkbook register.

Con: I wasn't just gambling with my future—I had my child's well-being to consider. One wrong move could alter our lives for the worse. My boy deserved a solid, decent life, and it was my job to make sure he got it, and frankly, I was the only one who would make it a priority.

This wasn't just a decision; it was a crossroads. And I was terrified.

I quietly folded my hands. "Father," I prayed, "You didn't bring me this high to drop me, but right now, I need absolute clarity. You are going to have to speak audibly because I need to be sure."

I talk to God a lot—and now, I pictured Jesus Himself, situated on the foot of my borrowed full-sized bed, heaped with blankets that were warm, even if nothing matched. It was a long, long way from my upper-middle class, private school upbringing south of Nashville. "I am putting this at your feet, Lord. Help me."

Silence. Dead silence. "God?"

I shook my head, and got up to start a load of laundry. I tried to put the weight of the decision out of my mind as my handsome boy, all of 17 and full of big ideas and every last drop of the tenacity afforded to our entire family, sauntered into my room to talk. I love him dearly, but weeks of being home together in the wake of the COVID-19 virus had become stifling for us both.

"What'cha going to do, Mom?"

"I don't know, babe. It's a lot of money, and we don't have it."

"You have your emergency fund."

"This is not an emergency." …But maybe it was an emergency. Maybe it was the same as running a Hail Mary. What would Dave Ramsey say? I shook my head. Dave Ramsey would hate this. My stomach turned.

For all the horrible, hard choices that I'd had to make in the last four years—and so many that demanded so much more gravity than this one, I hated having to make this particular choice with everything in me. It wasn't that I didn't want it, it was that I had been conditioned to serve at all costs, and this seemed boldly selfish on so many levels.

"Mom," he prodded, "I think you have to do it."

Reluctantly, I swallowed my feelings and followed the advice. I started my own ad agency.

***

Author's Note: I first named the agency *Kellum Creek Creative*, after the quiet road that led to the little frame house on a less-than-quarter-acre lot I had bought in my very own name when I was young. That little house and its mortgage were among the few things I retained when my marriage ended. But even then, God—in his quiet, unwavering way—was already making a way for me and my son.

Today, the business is called *Kellum Creek Business Solutions.* We hadn't achieved much yet when I decided to change the name. The work was still small, still scrappy. But something in me was shifting. I wanted to build more than just creative projects—I wanted to solve problems, offer real solutions, and help others build what they dreamed of. So, I renamed it *Kellum Creek Business Solutions*—not because we had arrived, but because I was finally beginning to see where we were going.

The day I turned the key on my building- my very own advertising agency- my stomach was rife with butterflies—a little like being head over heels in love, and yet not unlike the terror you feel during a slow build to the climax of a murder thriller. Like so many women I've talked to since, there was something in me nudging me towards something important, a way to serve my community, benefit my family—as little and broken as it was—and leave a mark. The onset of that journey (as much as I prayed for clarity) was murky most times at best. I lacked the one thing that I longed for, and arguably needed most desperately: a guide, someone to encourage me, caution me, and tell me what would work and what wouldn't, someone in my ear, whispering, "You've got this, just don't misstep and fall off that ledge." It made me miss my mama something fierce.

While I'm not your mama, I hope that this book helps quell some of the terror you may be feeling right now as you contemplate opening your own business or make the next best decision, business or otherwise, for your future. It's the lexicon I wished I'd had, crafted from lots of hard lessons, my fair share of mistakes, and the grace that God has allowed over it all. As a Christian, a Southern woman, an Army mom, and a small-town business owner, I've faced challenges that are undeniably unique, but I am confident the weight of trials and struggles will resonate with my sisters near and far who have always had an inkling that they were meant to build something extraordinary.

This is more than just a business book; it's a story of faith and service and purpose. I hope it inspires you enough to dream big and offers enough good advice to help you create a roadmap, bolster it with all the wisdom you can garner from all the best places, and perhaps, most of all, know that you are not in this alone.

Yes, mama, I see you, and I know your worry. Yes, I've been exactly where you are. I've left a relationship marked by fear and isolation. I've prayed about where the next meal would come from. I've done it because sometimes good women must make hard choices, and because I needed to remember who I was, and for that little flicker of hope that refuses to be doused. Looking back, I realize I also did it so I could tell you my story, so it could be your blueprint, a handbook of sorts for how to keep it all together and, hopefully, how to thrive. Hang on tight, friend. Let me assure you, God's plan is so much bigger than you can possibly imagine. Are you ready? Here we go.

See, I am doing a new thing! Now it springs up; do you not perceive it? -Isaiah 43:19

Chapter 1

Where I Come From

My childhood had some turbulence. I knew early that there was evil in the world—real, unrepentant cruelty that didn't wait for you to grow up to find you. But even then, I also knew there was good. So much good it could break your heart, if you let it. I knew it in flashes—a kind teacher's hand on my back, a chocolate meringue pie cooling on my Mamaw's dryer, the way my mother made up songs while she folded laundry. But nowhere was that goodness more palpable, more soul-filling, than at my Nana's home.

Her house was a sanctuary tucked deep in the soybean fields of Northeast Arkansas, rooted on land that had belonged to her father, now tended by her beloved brother, my great Uncle Jimmy. That stretch of earth felt like the edge of the world and the center of it all at once. You could stand on the back porch at dusk and watch the sun melt into the soybeans, lighting the fields on fire with gold. I can still hear the crickets humming like a gospel choir, and the rustle of the wind moving through those fields like it had secrets to tell if you were quiet enough to listen.

I spent countless hours at Nana's laminated wood-look kitchen table, where the food was good, but the conversation was better. There was magic in that kitchen—the kind that didn't come from potions but from patience, prayer, and the exact right amount of

Crisco that never touched a measuring cup. She made everything taste like home, even when nothing else did. I'd sit hungry for time to talk to her at that table while she told me stories from her childhood, or just looked at me with those sharp, knowing eyes that made you feel both completely seen and gently protected.

Across the carport was my Uncle Jimmy and Aunt Neva's house, and it was its own kind of heaven. There was always a basketball game on TV, fish frying in the skillet with a sizzle that sang of Saturday nights, and cold, sweet watermelon waiting near the screen door to the carport like it had been expecting me. Uncle Jimmy would crack a joke just to hear you laugh, and Aunt Neva had a way of smiling a knowing smile that made you feel like everything was going to be alright--even if it wasn't.

When they told me to go play outside, I was handed the keys to a kingdom. I had the run of the fields, wide open and humming with life. A four-wheeler became my chariot once I was big enough to ride it on my own, and a rotating cast of good dogs—all Australian Shepherds named "Chigger," — followed me like shadows. Those dogs were smart and loyal and incredibly funny. We'd ride down dirt paths until the sky turned that peculiar blue-gray of late evening, and then head to the house where I watched the stars climb back into place.

Church was as steady a rhythm in my life as the changing of seasons. My mother was a devoted member of the local Assembly of God, where tambourines rang like battle cries and speaking in tongues felt like stepping into the wildness of Heaven. On other Sundays, my Nana would take me to the Church of Christ, where reverence was a quiet thing—no instruments, no clapping, just human voices lifted in raw harmony that could rattle the soul. I loved both. Between them, I grew up steeped in stories of the Maker. Back then, I could quote you chapter and verse, hand raised high in Sunday School with the kind of confidence that only comes from not yet being tested.

But I would come to know God differently later on — in the kind of valley you don't walk through so much as belly crawl. The kind where your breath feels borrowed and your faith is held together with trembling, weak hands. Looking back, I believe He allowed it. Maybe even ordained it. That's another part of my story, one I'm not often tempted to revisit as necessary as it sometimes is.

I was an awkward child--pudgy, sometimes too loud, and often lost in my own head. I lived more on the page than I did in the world. I wrote everything down. It was the one place where I could be as loud or as quiet as I wanted to be without apology. But when it came time to speak those words out loud, especially in front of other children, I often choked. The words stayed lodged in my throat like stones.

We moved often—transience wrapped in cardboard boxes and tearful goodbyes. My father's work changed where we called home every few years, and while some towns felt like unexpected gifts, others felt like punishment. It's strange how much power people have in shaping a place. The right ones welcome you in and give you a soft place to land. The wrong ones make you dread the walk to school and learn how to shrink yourself, so you don't draw fire. I knew both kinds. And it was the wrong ones who taught me fear—real, body-deep fear that followed me into my dreams and shaped the way I saw myself for years to come.

I believe I was about thirteen when we landed in a picturesque neighborhood just south of Nashville—a place that looked like it had been plucked right out of a Southern Living magazine, all manicured lawns and brick mailboxes, the smell of fresh pavement still clinging to the cul-de-sac. My father had taken a new position with his company—something to do with investigating arsons, and my mother, Mo, was thrilled to be teaching math at a private school so polished and prestigious, you'd have thought they were molding the next cabinet of the POTUS.

"Mo" was the name I had lovingly, and somewhat maliciously, assigned her. It started as a joke—one of those offhand teenaged moments meant to needle, to reclaim a sliver of control in a world shifting too fast under my feet. But it stuck. And, to my great delight, it made her twitch every time I used it.

Mo was over the moon about our new life. She practically beamed when she told me I'd be attending "one of the finest academies in the entire Southeast." I, however, was not beaming. I was thirteen, hormonal, and freshly devoted to the gods of heavy metal. I had recently discovered the sacred trinity of Def Leppard,

Metallica, and Motley Crüe—and with them, a sudden, unshakable fascination with boys who played guitars, wore leather jackets, and sported hair teased up to the heavens like an '80s altar to chaos itself. I had no interest in sitting up straight in a plaid skirt and pretending I liked learning how to diagram sentences.

So, in my infinite teenaged wisdom, I did what any self-respecting rebel-in-the-making would do: I made that summer a living hell for Mo. If she wanted a charming, compliant daughter with a love for calculus and cardigans, she was going to have to look elsewhere. I rolled my eyes with Olympic precision. Slammed doors like it was a competitive sport (as long as my dad wasn't within earshot). I told her, in no uncertain terms, that if anyone made me wear a uniform, I would turn my teenage wrath on the entire state of Tennessee. Misery, in my opinion back then, should be a shared experience.

And let me tell you—I wasn't just sassy. I was awful. I was mean and magnetic. I had the kind of smile that made grown women second guess themselves, and boys suddenly forget their locker combinations. I was a cocktail of brains, beauty, and full-throttle defiance. And I knew it.

My mother—ever the gentle but exhausted educator—tried every trick in her toolkit to peel back the armor I was so determined to keep welded to my skin. She offered me bribes disguised as "rewards." She sat on the edge of my bed with soft eyes and stories about how hard girlhood can be, how she understood. Sometimes, I caught her staring at me like she was remembering the version of me that used to reach for her hand instead of yanking it away.

But one day, she got clever. Or lucky. Maybe both.

His name was Brandon. He had dark, tousled hair with inquiring eyes, vaguely resembling a young Joaquin Phoenix, and apparently, was a regular churchgoer. He was everything a Southern mother could dream of: polite, clean-cut, and armed with a killer smile and a Bible. And just like that, my mother's prayers took on a pulse. She saw a glimmer of hope… and she pounced.

That's how the Burnette clan became new members of Oak Valley Baptist Church. The sanctuary was small, the choir was earnest, and it just so happened to be brimming with teenage boys—boys who didn't wear uniforms, who smelled like cologne and sawdust, who played three chords on second-hand Fenders and made you believe music might actually be a religion.

It was the little church that became my refuge—a contradiction to the stiff-collared, reputation-obsessed world of the posh private school that now filled my days. The academy that taught me to think critically and made the writer I am today had pristine hallways and pressed khakis, locker rooms that smelled like soap and bleach and whispered secrets. Girls who looked as if they belonged in catalogues, who knew the exact shade of lip gloss that matched their privilege. I, in all my angst and too much eyeliner, felt like a rogue element. A walking rebellion with a backpack full of notebooks, song lyrics scribbled in the margins of math homework, and a stubborn refusal to fit in.

But Oak Valley Baptist— that place felt like freedom. It smelled like old pews and potluck dinners, of musty hymnals and Drakkar body spray worn entirely too enthusiastically by the boys who filed into youth group like they were walking onto a stage. And to be honest, in a way, they were. Every church lock-in, every fifth-Sunday singalong, every Sunday night service—they were performances of another kind. Less polished, more raw. And I ate it up like communion.

More than a handful of those boys—most of them raised on dusty roads and classic rock—won my attention without even trying. It wasn't just the music, though the sound of a half-tuned Fender guitar being plucked during worship rehearsal still makes my chest ache a little. It was the way they moved, the quiet confidence of kids who weren't trying to impress anyone—least of all the preacher standing at the back of the sanctuary with a Bible under his arm and skepticism in his eyes. These boys smoked their daddys' cigarettes behind the fellowship hall and still managed to show up early to carry folding chairs inside. They could quote scripture and Skynyrd in the same breath.

They wore their rebellion like a second skin—ripped jeans hanging low on narrow hips, Guns N' Roses T-shirts so worn they looked like heirlooms. Shirts their mamas probably hadn't seen since laundry day, if ever. Their voices were deep with that scratch of early manhood, and they laughed in a way that made me believe they didn't have a care in the world. That kind of freedom? It was magnetic. It was intoxicating. And it became the gravitational pull around which my whole teenage universe started to spin.

So, I gave myself over to it—the music, the glances passed like notes during altar call, the sticky warmth of July youth nights where I'd sneak out of the sanctuary and stand under the stars with a boy who smelled like leather and summer rain. They'd hand me a pick and teach me chords, or let me trace the names carved into the wood of the church picnic tables while we talked about everything and nothing. That became my altar.

My energy, once scattered and sharp-edged, found a new kind of focus. I wasn't interested in honors classes or yearbook committees. I was chasing something louder, messier, more alive. I started dressing to be noticed, when I wasn't bound to dress code. Black nail polish and ripped jeans were the fabric of my rebellion like incense in a cathedral. I knew what I was doing. And I knew it was driving Mo to her knees.

I would hear her some nights—in the hallway outside my bedroom. Her voice low, desperate. My name falling from her lips in prayer like it was too heavy to carry in silence anymore. "God, please," she'd whisper, her grief tangled with hope. "Don't let her slip away."

Sometimes I'd pause with one foot sliding into my favorite Doc Martens or fingers hovering over my stereo, caught between the sharp pang of guilt and the wild hum of independence. I never told her I heard her. I never told her that somewhere, deep down, I wanted to be saved— but not from the boys or the music or the feelings I couldn't yet name. I wanted to be saved from the ache of not knowing who I was, from the constant sense that I was too much and not enough all at once.

Oak Valley didn't fix me. It didn't make me good. But it gave me a place to breathe. To be loud. To be noticed. And maybe that was enough for a while.

Oak Valley Baptist Church, for all its humble charm and fraying hymnals, managed to keep a toehold on even the wildest among us. It was the kind of place that didn't demand perfection, just asked that you show up. And somehow, we did. We traded the dizzy, electric freedom of our Friday nights—the basement shows, the bonfires, the tailgate confessions—for quiet promises whispered to our mothers: "Yes, I'll be there Sunday." Sometimes it was a deal struck over pancakes or through a raised eyebrow from across the dinner table. Sometimes it was guilt. Sometimes it was love. But we all came.

We met in the basement of a house church without a church building, like a hidden heartbeat. The whole place couldn't have held more than two hundred souls on a good day.

The basement walls were painted an unremarkable beige, scuffed by years of folding chairs and restless feet. The carpet was the color of dust and outdated bulletin boards filled the foyer with hand-colored memory verses. And still, despite our best efforts to be unimpressed, a little bit of God trickled down to us.

It wasn't fire and brimstone. It wasn't conversion by fear. It was smaller than that. Gentler. Like water working its way through stone—persistent, quiet, sacred.

A slow saturation. Seeds got planted there—between the soda machines and the acoustic guitars, in the echoes of bad jokes and whispered prayers.

They took root in the middle of our chaos. They grew in the margins—in the laughter after lights-out at lock-ins, in the long car rides to youth conferences where we talked about everything but Jesus until someone cried, and then we all did. They grew in the moments when someone's parents split up, or someone's brother got arrested, and we showed up with extra cigarettes and fast food and silence, because sometimes that's all a 15-year-old knows how to give. But it was enough. Somehow, it was always enough.

That church basement, with its flickering fluorescent lights and folding chairs, became our sanctuary. Our proving ground. Our confession booth. Our recovery room. We were all a little broken, and none of us wanted to admit it, but Oak Valley held us anyway. It held our questions. Our doubts. Our stubborn, aching hope.

And years later, when the noise of the world got louder — when marriages faltered, when dreams unraveled, when faith slipped through my fingers like water — I would remember the stillness of those Sunday mornings. The quiet hum of the old furnace. The familiar voices singing just a little off-key. I'd remember how it felt to be held in a place that asked nothing more than, "Just come."

I have no doubt that God was in those rooms. Maybe not always in the sermons. Maybe not always even in the music. But in the laughter, in the friendships, in the unspoken understanding between kids who were all just trying to find some footing in the in-between—that's where the divine lingered.

And long after I stopped calling Oak Valley my church, I never stopped calling it home.

I've never liked the word balance. It always felt sterile to me, like something found on a therapist's worksheet or the cover of a self-help book that promises peace in three easy steps. But Oak Valley gave me balance in the most God-sent, real, breathing way. Not balance in the sense of perfection or predictability, but in the sense of sacred rhythm. The way a song builds, crashes, and then rests in a quiet refrain.

I loved the noise of Friday nights—the sound of a guitar amp crackling to life, the drums kicking like a heartbeat too big for a ribcage, the way music filled your whole body and left you both exhausted and somehow more alive.

But I also loved the slow ache of Sunday mornings. The old hymns, the creak of those cold folding chairs under worn-out bodies. I loved the way the light filtered through the dust in the air, like the Spirit moving in plain sight.

And while I bucked the private school classroom, I couldn't help but fall in love with learning. Not the kind measured by scantrons and report cards, but the kind that made me want to dig deeper. I found myself drawn to hard work, even when I pretended I wasn't. Whether it was rolling up my sleeves to scrape and paint an old, weather-beaten trailer on a youth service day, or spending hours revising a single paragraph in a story no one had asked me to write—I was learning what it meant to pour yourself into something.

The words… oh, the words. They came like a river, uninvited and unstoppable. They filled journals I hid under my bed, scrawled themselves into margins of notebooks, spilled onto church bulletins and receipts. I wrote essays with too much heart and short stories that turned into half-formed novels I never finished. My first book attempt was a spectacular failure, but it didn't matter. The writing wasn't about being good. It was about staying sane.

What made Oak Valley truly holy, though, wasn't the building or the music or even the sermons. It was the people. My people. The kids who took me in without flinching, who didn't care that I preferred holes in my jeans or sang tone-deaf harmony like it was my birthright. We all had that little church in common, nestled between two sleepy suburban neighborhoods, and it became our heartbeat. I made friends and was attending church regularly. My parents sighed some relief.

…Until I announced that I was going into missions.

And until the moment I announced I was going into missions, things in my life were...tense, but manageable. That announcement, though—it set off a chain reaction I wasn't entirely prepared for.

The call I felt wasn't whimsical or fleeting. It was heavy. It pressed against my chest like a weight I couldn't put down, handed to me by the Almighty Himself. A divine burden wrapped in clarity. And when I spoke it aloud, when I said I believed God was calling me to go, the reaction was immediate and fierce. Chaos, like a sudden storm in an already uneasy sky.

There were sharp words and slammed doors, gnashing of teeth both literal and metaphorical. My parents—bless them —believed wholeheartedly that I had lost my mind. My father, a man who didn't usually question my faith, looked at me with concern that bordered on fear. He asked if I was sure it was God's voice I was hearing, and not some fever dream of idealism or emotional confusion. My mother, tired and scared, cried. Not from joy or pride, but from raw, aching frustration.

I was sixteen by then. Fierce, stubborn, and full of what I believed was holy fire. But in truth, I was trembling under it all. The noise, the resistance, the doubt—it got to me. So, I did what I only sometimes remembered to do back then. I dropped to my knees.

And that's when it came—not thunder, not lightning, not a scroll from the heavens. Just one word. So small I nearly missed it. But it rang clear, cutting through the storm in my heart like a steady bell.

"Wait."

So, I did.

Chapter 2

When God Says Now

Another fifteen years passed. Life happened. I worked jobs I didn't love. I made mistakes that scarred me. I loved, I lost, I grew. And then, out of the quiet, God showed up again. This time not with a whisper, but a pull. An actual tug at the deepest part of me. He hadn't forgotten the promise I made at sixteen. He was calling it in.

The timing, by every logical standard, was a disaster. Everything in my life was mid-step, half-baked, or falling apart. But somehow, even in the wreckage, it was blessed.

Because when God says now, He means it. Even if you've already packed your excuses in neatly labeled boxes. Even if the ground under you is shaking.

Sometimes, obedience doesn't look like brave declarations. Sometimes, it looks like waiting. And sometimes, it looks like finally saying yes, even when it hurts.

My mission field wasn't some far-off land or exotic calling. It was tucked into the folds of the Appalachian Mountains, inside a humble medical and dental clinic that served people who had long been overlooked. I was hired into a role I had no real qualifications for — at least not on paper—but I thrived. We cared for folks who had no access to primary medical or dental care, and I made it my business to raise the funds that kept those doors open. I was good at it. Exceptionally good. For the first time in a long time, life felt like it was falling into place.

I was married to my college sweetheart. I was a mother. I had a job that didn't just pay the bills; it lit a fire in me. I was surrounded by people of faith, where talk of God wasn't whispered in corners but welcomed into every meeting, every hallway conversation. We prayed together, worked shoulder to shoulder, and poured ourselves out for a cause bigger than ourselves. These weren't just coworkers—they became fast friends and fellow warriors for a mission we believed in.

And then, as life often does, it unraveled.

After several years of what felt like trying to build something meaningful—both at work and at home—I made the excruciating decision to leave my marriage. It wasn't sudden, but there came a turning point when there was no alternative but to walk away. I had held on for a long time, twisting myself into knots trying to "do the right thing." But the truth was, our marriage wasn't rooted in faith. And in the silence of my most desperate prayers, God showed up—not gently, not quietly, but with force. He protected me while everything else crumbled.

My work became a sanctuary. Those same coworkers — those people of faith—became my borrowed family. They held me together with coffee, prayer, and quiet companionship when I couldn't hold myself. The mission kept me grounded, and in the midst of the storm, God kept providing.

I agreed not to pursue child support. I just wanted peace. But peace came with its own cost.

Not long after, the clinic changed hands. My manager-- the one who had seen potential in me before I saw it in myself—retired, and leadership shifted. I had hoped, prayed even, to step into her shoes. But another was chosen, and my new boss made it abundantly clear, in subtle and not-so-subtle ways, that it would be best if I moved on.

But I wasn't ready to move. I had a son still in school. No savings after the legal ordeal. No safety net, only this job that had once been a calling but was quickly becoming a cage. So, I stayed. I prayed. I begged God to fix things—to soften hearts, to open doors, to give me a sign. Anything.

And God, in His infinite mercy and mischief, answered.

It is always a hard lesson when you learn to be careful what you pray for.

COVID-19 hit like a tidal wave—sudden, merciless, and indiscriminate. It didn't just change the world; it carved through mine like a storm, uprooting everything I thought was stable. The clinic, once a place of purpose and belonging, began to shift beneath my feet. I was no longer the golden child, no longer the one everyone rallied around. My new boss rarely spoke to me.

The staff turned over rapidly during those early pandemic days. One by one, the people I'd leaned on, prayed with, fought beside—they left. And each goodbye chipped away at the home I'd built there. The walls grew quieter, the mission murkier. I stayed, but I felt like a ghost of the woman who once walked those halls with purpose.

After every clinic shift, I drove to a local luxury hotel where I worked the front desk, standing under soft lights in a polished lobby, pretending to be composed. It was the only way I could keep the bills paid. But in the in-between—the drive from the clinic to the hotel—I unraveled.

I cried every evening. Not the quiet kind of crying, either. The kind that makes your chest hurt and your soul ache. The kind that leaves salt stains on your steering wheel. And in those moments, when I couldn't see the way forward, I did the only thing that made sense.

I prayed.

Not with eloquent words or lengthy pleas. My prayer was simple. Desperate. Repetitive: "God, change things."

He came through with flying colors.

That year, despite everything—despite the upheaval, the tears, the late-night hotel shifts—I'd raised *a lot* of money. Maybe more than in any other year on record, thanks to those who wanted to somehow help with the raging pandemic. I kept my head down, bit my tongue more times than I could count, and walked on eggshells so often my soul felt bruised. I told myself this was just a season. That if I could stay quiet and keep working hard, things would level out.

Eventually, I began to believe they had.

When we returned to the office after the lockdown, I let myself exhale just enough to step away from my second job at the hotel. I was exhausted, and for the first time in a long while, I thought maybe I could breathe. Maybe things were starting to look up.

I went out of my way to extend kindness to my new boss. Not just polite nods in the hallway, but intentional gestures—coffee when she looked tired, surprise treats for the office, a donation to a charity she cared about. I complimented her when I could find the space to do so with integrity. I was determined to build a bridge, to make something work out of the broken pieces we'd been handed.

And all the while, I prayed.

One particular prayer kept circling back in my spirit, something Mo taught me when I was younger: *God, if this isn't right, close the door.*

Did I already say to be careful what you pray for?

Because without warning, without a whisper of what was coming, I was called into an office on a random weekday at 2 p.m. and fired. No ceremony. No explanation. Just… done.

Shaken doesn't begin to cover it. I was gutted.

There I stood—officially a single, unemployed mother in the middle of a global pandemic with less than a week's worth of groceries in the pantry. Unemployment systems were overwhelmed and weeks behind. The local office offered me little more than a sympathetic shrug and a warning: It would be several months before my case was even reviewed for benefits.

My prayers didn't bring lightning bolts or quick answers. There was no miraculous check in the mail, no sudden job offer wrapped in gold. What came instead were long, lonely nights at the kitchen table, lit by the soft glow of my laptop, as I wrote and studied and hustled my way through an uncertain future.

I had no idea how we would make it. I've never felt so low and so helpless. Sometime before, I'd started an online master's program because I was fairly certain that not being promoted to head of the Clinic had something to do with my lack of a graduate degree. To keep my mind in a better place, I doubled down on my classes, borrowed some additional funds to make certain we could eat, began charting a course for better days, and took on as much freelance writing as possible. Somewhere in the mix, I started listening to a guy named Dave Ramsey on the radio. He said I needed to scrimp together a $1,000 emergency fund—so I did. I also kept praying.

I built a new kind of rhythm—one stitched together with resilience and ramen, hope and overdue bills. I stayed up late editing content, writing book reviews, and crafting product descriptions while trying to fund survival. I took every job that came my way—big or small, glamorous or gritty. Nothing was beneath me, because survival doesn't come with an ego.

That emergency fund became more than just a number in a savings account; it became proof that I could still choose my future. That I wasn't done. That even in the absence of a steady paycheck, in the silence of unanswered prayers, I still had agency. I still had breath.

And God, in His own way, showed up—not through the kindness of an employer, but in the stillness of my determination. In the friends who delivered meals without being asked. In the way my son woke up singing happily if horribly off key after a night of hot tears rolling down my cheeks in the dark. In the flicker of peace that came when I closed my eyes and whispered, "I'm still here."

The ground was shaky, but it was still ground. And I was still standing.

I didn't know what was next. I didn't have a five-year plan. But I had just enough light for the next step. Just enough strength to keep showing up.

And that was enough.

For now.

I hadn't planned on staying long. I'd only stopped by Diantha Currier's place to pick up a few Mason jars she'd promised me months ago for a project I'd almost forgotten. But as soon as I stepped inside, she waved me toward the kitchen table, already pulling out an extra mug. That was Diantha—always ready with warmth and caffeine.

We'd become friends through the Rotary Club, a place where I'd first admired her from afar—her blunt, no-nonsense way of facing even the most daunting challenges head-on. She had a steadiness about her, like someone who had walked through fire and figured out how to carry the smoke like perfume.

It felt good to be in her kitchen, even if I hadn't meant to end up there that day. The kind of good that wraps around your tired bones and says *you don't have to be strong here.*

We sat and talked. About being single mothers raising boys who were trying to become good men. About retirement dreams and whether they ever really arrive. About how the Rotary Club had changed over the years. About resilience—and how some people come through the hard times polished and others just come through scarred.

Diantha always had a soft spot for my son. She'd fussed over him when he was younger, always asking how he was doing with school or sports. That day, she wove his name into our conversation like a thread meant to keep me anchored. She told me I was doing fine, that he was turning out just right.

And then she cut to the chase, like only Diantha could.

"So, what do you want to do?" she asked, casually, like she was offering a second cup of coffee.

I blinked. "What do you mean, what do I want to do?" The question felt absurd. "I need a job, Diantha. I need something that pays the bills. And I need it fast." She knew this. Everyone who knew me knew this.

She just looked at me, unmoved. "I didn't ask what you need. I asked what you want to do."

I went quiet. My brain, already tired from the constant loop of worry, short-circuited.

"If you could do anything," she pressed, her eyes suddenly sharp and soft at the same time, "what would it be?"

And without even thinking—without weighing the cost, without censoring it through practicality—the words slipped out like they'd been waiting.

"I'd open an advertising agency."

She didn't flinch. Didn't laugh or offer a hundred reasons why it wouldn't work. Instead, she grinned that wide, knowing grin of hers and said, "Then you need to get on that. You're not getting any younger."

I laughed—because what else do you do when someone dares to believe in your dreams more than you've let yourself?

I gathered my jars and headed home, telling myself it was just a pipedream. A fantasy whispered between two friends in a warm kitchen.

But the thing about Diantha?

She didn't traffic in pipedreams.

She handed out blueprints.

Chapter 3

One Foot in Front of the Other

*You'll never do a whole lot unless you're brave enough
to try.* -Dolly Parton

My phone buzzed at the worst possible moment, as if it
had a sixth sense for chaos. It always seems to ring when
your hands are full, your heart is heavy, or you're just
one inconvenience away from unraveling. I glanced at
the screen and saw the name: Diantha.

It took a second for it to register. We hadn't spoken in a
while, life had been crowded, and the pandemic had
elbowed out all but the most essential contact. No
kitchen table chats. No jars exchanged. Just silence,
thick with distance.

"I found your office!" she announced before I could even
say hello, skipping over every customary greeting like
they were speed bumps in her rush to get to the point.

I sighed, pinching the bridge of my nose. "I don't have
an office, Diantha. I barely have a desk. I have a corner
of a kitchen table that doubles as a bill-paying station
and a coffee spill zone."

But I knew that tone. The one that said she wasn't
making a suggestion—she was planting a flag.

"You need to see this," she pressed, her voice dancing with certainty. "It's for rent, and it's perfect. You can finally open your advertising agency."

The words landed like a punch and a promise at the same time. *Finally open your agency.* As if that dream I barely dared to whisper had always been waiting, just around a corner I didn't have the nerve to turn.

My first instinct wasn't hope—it was panic. My finances were so tight I rationed toothpaste. The idea of committing to rent on a commercial space felt laughable, irresponsible. And yet… I also knew Diantha. When she caught wind of something she believed in, she didn't let it go. And I didn't want to be the ungrateful friend who brushed off her relentless hope.

She rattled off the address and a few quirky details, her voice full of sparkle. As she talked, that familiar knot twisted tighter in my stomach. I hung up, hesitated—and then, against every practical bone in my body, I stepped outside and started the car.

The little blue Hyundai—a sacrifice purchased for my son, now mine out of necessity—coughed to life. I drove slowly, every turn a silent argument with myself. The place was only five miles away, but five miles feels a lot farther when you're driving toward a dream that's always scared you. I kept waiting for common sense to win, for my hands to turn the wheel back home. But I had promised Diantha. And somehow, that mattered more than fear.

When I finally pulled up, my breath caught.

It was a little building on Forks of the River Parkway in Sevierville. I knew the place, had passed it countless times without ever seeing it. Now, with Diantha's eyes in my head, I noticed the "For Lease" sign crooked in the window. The building was modest, almost invisible—an old tattoo parlor, by the look of it—but it had a kind of stubborn charm. Like it knew how to stay put.

I sat there for a long moment, unsure of what to do next. Then I called the number on the sign. A warm voice answered. The current tenant, a woman moving her real estate office elsewhere, was nearby and happy to show me around. "Be there in a few," she said cheerfully.

As I tried to gather my scattered thoughts, my phone rang again. This time, it was my boy.

"What'cha doing, Mom?" His voice was easy, familiar. He always opened that way.

What was I doing? The honest answer was I had no clue. I was about to walk into a building I couldn't afford to dream about, on a whim sparked by a friend's wild hope. I was doing something so far outside my comfort zone, it felt like I needed permission just to breathe.

But I didn't deflect. I didn't lie.

Instead, I told him where I was and why.

"I'm coming to see it with you," he said without hesitation.

Just like that, the universe shifted. My son—my steady, observant boy—was on his way. He was coming to bear witness to the moment his mother cracked the door open to possibility.

And there I sat, in a weathered parking lot outside an unremarkable building, with my heart pounding like it was trying to escape. The air was thick with maybe. And I could almost hear Diantha's voice in my head: *You're not getting any younger.*

This wasn't just a detour. This was the beginning of something.

***

Writing that first check wasn't just a business transaction—it was a soul-deep reckoning. A reckoning with every version of myself that had ever dreamed, and every one that had dared not to.

That slip of paper, modest and crisp, carried more than dollar signs. It carried childhood dreams I'd tucked away for decades, dreams I'd folded so tightly they had creases like old maps. From the time I could string sentences together, I'd wanted to be in advertising. While other kids played house or doctor, I was staging mock commercials for school supplies, turning my Lisa Frank folders into product pitches, narrating the virtues of Trapper Keepers and erasable pens in the singsong cadence of a jingle.

I was a less-than-remarkable little girl who filled the margins of her notebooks with imaginary taglines and names of boys who barely knew I existed—scribbled side by side, hope and longing tangled together in adolescent ink.

And then life happened.

Those dreams were smothered under layers of practicality, silenced in a marriage that made no room for dreaming, let alone creating. I convinced myself stability was the right trade-off. I buried those ambitions in the steady rhythm of nonprofit work, trading in my voice for a cause. And when even that unraveled, the dreams felt too far gone to resurrect.

But here I was. Pen in hand. Heart pounding. Writing a check from the emergency fund I'd painstakingly built, dollar by hard-earned dollar, just to keep the lights on and food in the fridge. This wasn't just my money—it was my safety net, my Plan B, C, and D.

Dave Ramsey would've had a conniption. And I wouldn't have blamed him.

Because what kind of sane woman takes her emergency fund and hands it over to lease an office for a business she hasn't even launched yet? A woman with no financial backing, no guarantees, and a mountain of fear?

Apparently, me.

My hand shook as I signed my name. The weight of it all—the risk, the audacity, the dream—settled in my stomach like a stone. It felt reckless. It felt exhilarating. It felt… final.

Failure wasn't just an abstract idea. It was a living, breathing thing in the corner of the room, smirking at me, cataloging every reason this could go wrong: not enough clients, not enough experience, not enough me.

But for the first time in my life, I did the unthinkable. I stepped to the edge of the cliff and didn't turn around. I folded the check, handed it over, and told myself the truth I needed to believe:

You don't need to have all the answers to begin. Courage doesn't always feel like a lion's roar. Sometimes, it feels like nausea and second-guessing. Sometimes, it's just staying upright when every cell in your body wants to run.

And then—I went home and threw up.

Chapter 4

Beginnings

Dream big. Start small. But most of all, start.

– Simon Sinek

The sheer magnitude of what I'd done was almost too much to bear, but it was also somehow exhilarating.

There was nothing particularly glamorous about that office. The scent of disinfectant still clung faintly to the air, mixing with the dull hum of an ancient refrigerator that someone had graciously left behind. The space was small, neat, and a bit lonely. But it was also pretty. And more importantly, it was mine. Or at least, it was trying to be.

That first day, I perched in a borrowed office chair—one that had seen better decades—behind the same grad school laptop that had limped through too many assignments and not enough updates. I tried to see the place as it might be one day: furnished, alive, full of the kind of creative chaos that only comes from people believing in what they do.

But in that moment? It felt hollow. A shell waiting for proof that something meaningful might grow there.

As I hit "send" on the last freelance article in my assignments folder, the pride of checking a box was instantly replaced with a roar of self-doubt. What if I couldn't do this? What if all of this—the desk, the agency, the dream—was a grand delusion dressed up as ambition? The weight of it hit me hard. It wasn't just about income or rent. It was about belief—about the terrifying idea that I might not have what it takes after all.

My hands trembled as I stood. I locked the office door, got in the car… then got back out to double-check the lock. Old habits, born from old fears. I started the car, my mind looping through all the ways this could fall apart. It was so loud in my head I almost missed the most basic next step.

There was a dress shirt for my son waiting at the dry cleaner.

The smallest to-do sometimes becomes a lifeline.

I turned onto Honey Street and headed toward Hatcher's, clinging to that one thread of normalcy. When I pulled into the lot, there he was—Leonard Waring, the kind of small-town constant who somehow always shows up at the right moment. His smile broke through the haze I hadn't realized I'd been walking through all morning. His eyes held something gentle—an understanding, maybe even mourning—for what I'd lost when I was quietly pushed out of the clinic, the place where we'd once raised funds side by side for people like… well, like me now.

I swallowed hard. I hadn't wanted to explain myself to anyone, least of all someone who knew the "before" version of my life. But Leonard didn't press. Instead, he opened the door to something I didn't know I needed.

"I was sorry to hear about the clinic," he said, voice soft. "What are you doing now?"

I paused, trying to make the words real as I said them. "I've just opened an advertising agency on Forks of the River."

His whole face lit up. Not politely. Not pitifully. But genuinely.

"Well, that's great!" he beamed. "What would you think about doing some social media for us? We really need someone who knows about Facebook."

That was it. That was the moment. My first client.

It wasn't a national campaign or a billboard in Times Square. It was Facebook. For a Realtor.

I could've wept. I could've hugged him, though we weren't exactly on hugging terms. I could've dropped to my knees right there in the parking lot, overwhelmed with gratitude. Instead, I whispered, "Thank you, Father," under my breath and set a date to meet in my office—the one I still wasn't sure I could afford.

And just like that, something shifted. Hope cracked the door open again.

Beginnings are holy. Even the small ones. Especially the small ones. Write that down somewhere: Beginnings are holy.

I collected the starched white button-down from the counter, returned to the car, and sat there for a few quiet minutes, letting it all settle in. Before turning the key in the ignition, I whispered a second, quieter, "Thank you, Jesus."

The thing about starting over is this: every step feels like climbing a mountain in bare feet. The wind rips through you. Your breath freezes in your throat. The doubts gather like clouds. You're not just walking uphill, you're dragging every fear and failure behind you.

And yet…

Sometimes, if you're lucky, the universe sends you a smile in a dry cleaner's parking lot. A simple offer. A flicker of belief. A sign that says, *Keep going.*

Don't miss it. Don't miss the holy in the small. Don't miss the warm hand in the storm because you're too busy checking the weather.

Now, let's talk about Starting Small.

Because that? That's where the real stories begin.

Beginnings are a lot of things.

They're messy, humbling, exhilarating, and almost always more complicated than you planned. If anyone tells you that becoming a business owner is emotionally easy, brace yourself—they're either lying or selling something.

Starting a business is not for the faint of heart. And it sure as hell isn't for the half-committed. It demands everything. Your time, your sleep, your confidence, your tears. It asks for your full self, not the polished version with the clean resume, but the ragged, relentless version that doesn't quit even when the bank account begs you to.

You'll ride emotional highs so giddy they feel like jet fuel, only to crash into self-doubt so thick you can barely see straight. You'll feel proud and utterly inept in the same hour. There will be days when you walk into your office like a conquering hero… and days when you sit on the floor beside your desk and wonder what on earth made you think you could do this.

It's a roller coaster, friend. Buckle up. Or get off the ride.

Because this isn't a field for the easily discouraged or the casually involved. This is trench work. This is soul work.

And here's what you have to remind yourself, again and again: The highs and lows are normal. No two days will ever be the same. That's part of the beauty. And the beast.

Had a great first week? Fantastic. The second might suck. Land your dream client? She may become your biggest headache. Think you're finally ahead of the game? The market will remind you not to get cocky.

But the opposite is also true.

No money in the door this week? That doesn't mean next month won't break records. Buried in work and can't breathe? That might be the signal that it's time to hire— and when you find the right team, the magic begins. That project that went sideways and made you question everything? It's carving skills into you that no book or course ever could.

Let all of it shape you. Let it stretch you. Let it make you better—but don't let it steal your fire. Don't let it cloud your vision.

You have to start. That's the best advice I can give you, and it's also the terrifying, beautiful truth.

Start broke. Start afraid. Start with a heart that pounds in your chest and a voice that shakes when you say your dream out loud. Start at 25, 35, 45, or 60. Start even if your ducks aren't in a row; start even if one of your ducks is clearly a squirrel wearing a hat.

Start anyway.

Because if you don't? You'll never know the joy of the sunlight that follows a string of sleepless nights. You'll never know the satisfaction of saying, "I built this," or the heartbreak of trying again after a failure that could've flattened you—but didn't.

The point isn't perfection. It's motion.

So, go. Chase the thing. Fumble forward. Keep your eyes open for grace and grit and unexpected blessings. The path isn't linear (if it is, it's not authentic) but it's yours.

Doubting yourself does no good.

Very early on, I realized something was wrong—not with the business plan or the bank account, but with my own internal voice. The one that was supposed to cheer me on, push me forward, tell me I could do this? It was silent.

No whisper of confidence. No gentle nudge.

Just silence.

What should have been an inner monologue full of momentum and courage was completely drowned out by dread, years of self-doubt, and the quiet ache of never quite fitting in. My self-esteem wasn't just bruised—it was fractured. And I knew, deep in my bones, that I was utterly unworthy of anything that might even look like success.

And here's the thing: I know now I'm not alone.

That voice—or the absence of it—is heartbreakingly common. I've had the conversations. I've seen the shame show up in the eyes of others who've felt invisible, incapable, or fundamentally not enough. And I can testify to just how damaging that silence can be.

But hindsight, as they say, is 20/20.

Five years after writing that first terrifying reality check, I'd go back and say this to the woman I was then—and to you, if you need to hear it now:

Take care of your dream. Treat it like something sacred. Cling to it like a life raft. Because it is.

You are not here by accident. You don't have to earn your worth through success, or numbers, or the approval of people who never really saw you in the first place. You are as worthy as any other living, breathing, heart-thumping soul walking this earth. And if the King of Kings—Creator of galaxies and wildflowers—loves you as wildly and unconditionally as He does, then you owe it to yourself to love you, too.

I know what you're thinking. I know because I've been there.

How?

How can I be my own cheering section when I couldn't even sit at the right lunch table in high school?

How can I run a business when I couldn't even keep my marriage together?

How can I win at anything when I feel so utterly, irreparably broken?

Let me tell you something that changed everything for me: The answer isn't you. Not really. The answer is so much bigger. The answer is grace. The answer is God. He doesn't make mistakes.

So, if you need a roadmap, here's what I'd give you:

Start by breaking down your goals. Make them small. Achievable. Let them stack like steppingstones across the impossible. Don't get lost in the whole mountain when you can only see the first foothold. Keep moving inch by inch.

Pray over your work. Over your family. Over your dreams, your finances, your fears. Write them down. All of it. Get a journal that feels like home and spill everything in it. Remember what I said? *Write it out and lay it bare.* It still holds.

Prioritize the musts. Focus on what you can do today. And when you check something off your list, celebrate that. Be proud of that. Those little victories? They're not little at all.

And whatever you do, keep moving.

Don't let a bad day trick you into believing this isn't yours to do. Don't let a setback become a verdict. This is your time to shine—not the polished, perfect version of you, but the real one. The bruised and brilliant, healing and whole-making version.

Get rid of whatever you've been hiding behind. Step into the light—not because you've earned it, but because it's yours.

Meeting Leonard in that dry cleaner's parking lot was a Godsend. It wasn't flashy. It wasn't life-changing in the moment. But it was enough. Enough to tip the balance. Enough to help me choose courage over collapse. Enough to keep me moving forward when I wasn't sure I could.

In the grand scheme, it was a small thing. A little job. A social media gig that barely made a ripple on a spreadsheet.

But I'll tell you this: it mattered.

Since that day, Kellum Creek Business Solutions, the little agency that was once nothing but a fleeting dream, has grown. I've landed bigger clients, more exciting work, more complex campaigns that required me to stretch far beyond my comfort zone. But that first yes from Leonard? It was a cornerstone. A mustard seed of belief.

And I would be absolutely remiss if I didn't tell you how much that tiny win meant—not just to my morale, but to the future of this business.

So, here's what I've learned, and what I hope you remember:

- Look for good people. The ones who smile with their whole face. The ones who ask how you're really doing. The ones who show up in parking lots and boardrooms and inboxes with just enough grace to get you through the day.

- Find the handshakes and the kind eyes. Seek out the people who want you to win—not because it benefits them, but because they know what it's like to need a break. And when you find those people, don't let them go. They are the lifeblood of this whole journey.

And when the wins come—especially the small ones—celebrate them.

Celebrate them wildly and without shame.

Those little moments? They're not little. They're proof. Proof that progress is being made. Proof that your work matters, even when it doesn't trend or scale. Proof that you're building something that lasts.

Real success isn't always shiny. It doesn't always come with applause or headlines. More often, it shows up in the form of relationships forged in trust, in kindness, in mutual respect. The kind that deepens over time and create a kind of currency that money can't touch.

Because money isn't the whole story. In business, it's often just the side effect of a hundred people-centered wins, of small decisions made with integrity, of kindness offered when no one's looking.

So, celebrate the little jobs, the quiet victories, the Leonard moments.

That's where the good stuff lives.

Connections can change everything.

My friendship with Leonard was forged long before I ever imagined opening an advertising agency. We'd shared community events, conversations, and small kindnesses—the kind that layer over time to form something solid. I didn't know back then that his voice would become the lifeline I needed in one of my lowest moments. But it was. And that offer he made in the dry cleaner's parking lot? It didn't just give me a job—it gave me enough belief to keep stepping forward when I could barely find my footing.

That's what the right people do. They remind you who you are when you forget. They lend you courage when yours has run dry.

And you, my friend, need other people. Good people. People who believe in your talent and your purpose, even when you don't.

Some people say I know everyone in my hometown— and they're not far off. In a town of about 20,000 that swells with tourists year-round, I've learned who to call when your pipes burst, who bakes the world's best cinnamon rolls, and which dentist to see if you're squeamish about dental work.

But I didn't come by that knowledge overnight. I found those people. I showed up. I talked. I listened. I remembered names, asked follow-up questions, and said yes to more coffee dates than I had time for. Just like kids learn who to trust with their secrets and who not to sit beside during math class, I learned my people.

And the truth is, just because we grow up doesn't mean we stop needing our people. If anything, we need them more.

Your schoolyard is the world. Your peer group is humanity. Congratulations—and welcome to the most exhilarating, terrifying, and ultimately rewarding part of being a grown-up.

It should go without saying, but I'll say it loud anyway: Always be building and nurturing relationships.

Want to know the fastest way to build them? Serve people. Help where you can. Show up when it's inconvenient. Share your work with your network. Be generous with your knowledge and your encouragement.

Because here's the secret: when you serve others, they become invested in your success. And if you're lucky, some of them will link arms with you and help carry the dream when your arms are too tired to hold it alone.

This is what I tell my team: *Find your people.* It's not just good advice. It's survival.

Because when the timing's right, relationships built on trust and authenticity can blossom into business opportunities—and even more importantly, they'll reinforce the kind of reputation money can't buy.

And let's be honest, doing business with people you genuinely like? It's not just easier—it's more enjoyable. Dare I say... even profitable?

But let me also tell you this: not every client or customer who walks through your door is your person. And that's okay.

In the beginning, you will say yes to everyone. You'll take every project, every phone call, every questionable meeting. You'll smile through clenched teeth and tell yourself it's all part of paying dues.

But at some point, you'll feel that knot in your stomach. The one that shows up every time Mr. Brown calls, because you already know he's going to criticize, nitpick, or disrespect your time. Or Ms. Green, who turns every conversation into a monologue and never hears a word you say.

Let me give you permission right now: Let them go.

Wish them well. Be kind. Don't gossip. Help them find another provider if you can.

But let them go.

Here's a short but mighty list of when to release a client:

- If they're verbally or emotionally abusive.

- If they don't benefit from what you offer.

- If they don't understand—or respect—what you do.

- If they monopolize your time and drain your energy.

- If your gut says, "This isn't right."

- If they pick fights or make you question your competence.

Let them go.

Because here's the thing: Your peace is worth more than any paycheck. Your mission, your health, your joy—they deserve space to breathe. You cannot build something beautiful while dodging emotional landmines from the wrong people.

So, find your people. Celebrate the ones who cheer for you. Let go of the ones who don't.

And build something that matters—with people who remind you that you do, too.

Perspective comes from gratitude.

"Thanks" might seem too simple to warrant a place on a list of business essentials—but let me tell you, it belongs at the very top.

Never, ever forget to say thank you.

Say it when someone hires you. Say it when your friends send business your way. Say it to the family members who cheer you on or hold the fort when you're working late. Say it to the barista who knows your order and calls you by name on the mornings you feel invisible.

And most of all, say it to God. Say it every chance you get.

Thank Him for the blessings you can see—and the ones you can't. He's the reason any of this is moving forward. He is the one who makes a way when the road disappears. He can cover you with mercy and surround your work with favor. Or, if you forget Him, if you let pride slip in through the back door, He can humble you in a breath.

Gratitude is a spiritual posture. It's how you keep your heart soft and your vision clear.

And yes, I know—it's easier to be thankful when things are going well. When the invoices are paid, when the calls are returned, when the path is smooth. But what about when it's not? What about when the emails go unanswered, when the bills stack up, when your confidence slips through your fingers like water?

Even then—especially then—give thanks.

Because even when you're not earning, you're still learning. Even when the doors don't open, you're gathering strength. And those lessons, the hard-won ones that leave you raw and breathless? They're the ones that shape your grit and refine your calling.

Find the good in every circumstance. Yes, sometimes that means digging deep—deeper than you thought you could go. But dig anyway. Get your shovel. Gratitude is not optional. It's not a feel-good trend or a hashtag—it's the lifeline that keeps your soul tethered to what matters most.

And if gratitude doesn't come naturally to you—and for many, it doesn't—make it a practice. Build it into your rhythm. Each morning, before the noise of the day creeps in, take a few moments to whisper your thanks. And again, at night, when you're tempted to count worries instead of blessings, count blessings anyway.

Thank God for the tiny wins: the kind word, the paid invoice, the new idea, the moment of peace. Thank Him even in the middle of the mess. Because when you praise Him in the storm, something sacred happens.

Your eyes start to change. You begin to see differently. You start recognizing His providence in places you used to overlook.

And let me tell you—when that happens, when your heart starts bending toward gratitude, the blessings hit differently. They sink in deeper. They multiply.

Gratitude brings you closer to God.

And infinitely closer is exactly where you want to be when you're building something from the ground up. In fact, it's not just helpful—it's a necessity. And it's a privilege.

While beginnings are often fragile, uncertain, and laced with fear, they are also—perhaps more than any other time—the most important season of your business.

Yes, I've said it before, and I will say it again: treat your beginning with reverence.

There's a kind of holiness in these early days. A weight that doesn't just come from what you're building, but from who you're becoming in the process. These first steps—timid though they may feel—are laying the foundation for everything that will come after. For your future. For your team. For the lives your work will eventually touch.

You only get one beginning.

Don't rush it. Don't dismiss it as temporary or small. Don't reduce it to a scramble for sales or a frantic chase for approval.

Instead, approach this beginning like sacred ground.

Set clear goals, but let them come from your values, not just your fears. Don't aim only for profit—aim for purpose. Ask yourself what kind of leader you want to be, what kind of legacy you want your business to leave. Ask what kind of people you want to serve—and how you want to serve them.

These questions matter. Your answers matter.

Because this isn't just about the work. It never was.

It's about the relationships you build—with your team, your clients, your community. And yes, with God. Especially with God.

Because He's not just a silent observer in your business. He's in every decision, every conversation, every dollar earned or sacrificed. And the more you align your work with His purpose, the more peace you'll find in the process—even when the road is rough.

So, create good habits early. Build rhythms that serve your soul, not just your spreadsheet. Make time for prayer. For rest. For reflection. Let your calendar reflect your values, not just your deadlines.

This beginning is your chance to choose.

Choose integrity. Choose intention. Choose the kind of work you'll be proud of when all the noise fades away.

Because someday, you'll look back. You'll remember these fragile days—the long nights, the quiet fears, the small victories—and you'll be glad you didn't take them for granted.

Honor this beginning.

It is the ground on which everything else will rise.

Chapter 5

Opportunities

Opportunity doesn't always knock in heels and a blazer. Sometimes, it shows up with mud on its boots.

My great-uncle Jimmy was a farmer—salt-of-the-earth, steady hands, and the kind of man who understood that the best investments weren't always flashy, but necessary. One day, he made the trip from his rural farm into the city, intent on buying a new tractor. For those unfamiliar with the agriculture world, a tractor isn't just a tool. It's a livelihood. The price tag can rival a home or a barn—it's that essential.

When Uncle Jimmy arrived at the dealership, he wasn't the only one there. Sitting quietly, waiting for help, was another man—older, in faded overalls, his boots caked with dried mud. I used to picture him as the kind of man who had seen a thousand sunrises over fields he planted himself—weathered, bearded, and maybe a little overlooked.

And that's exactly what happened.

Salesperson after salesperson passed this man by. They greeted others in suits, others who looked the part of "real buyers." Meanwhile, the old farmer waited. No one saw the value sitting right there on that cracked leather bench.

Uncle Jimmy, who'd already made headway on his purchase, watched as a young, seemingly inexperienced sales associate finally approached the man in overalls. Within minutes, that same quiet man reached into his pocket and pulled out a thick roll of hundred-dollar bills. Cash. He didn't flinch. He paid in full for the most expensive tractor on the lot. Then he left, boots still muddy, dignity intact.

And the seasoned sales pros? They were left blinking in disbelief.

This story has stuck with me my entire life. And it came rushing back years later as I navigated my own path in business.

I've met with clients who arrived polished, credentials in hand, seemingly brimming with budget. Yet when it came time to commit, they disappeared faster than a Wi-Fi signal on a country road. And then there were others—people who looked scrappy, maybe a little uncertain, who walked in without fanfare. They didn't just hire me—they paid upfront, valued my expertise, and referred others.

Here's the truth I wish someone had tattooed on my entrepreneurial heart from day one: Don't judge capacity by appearance. Don't measure potential by polish. And never, ever assume someone can't afford you just because they don't match your vision of a "dream client."

Money doesn't always wear designer styles. Influence doesn't always speak perfect English. And loyalty doesn't always arrive in a luxury car.

As women in business, we're often taught to chase the dream client, the ideal avatar. But what if the real gold is in the unexpected conversations, the ones we almost skipped?

Stay open. Be adaptable. Build the relationship before you assess the return.

Because that man in overalls? He's out there. She's out there. And if we're paying attention—not just to wallets, but to people—we won't miss them.

Here's a secret: Struggle is the best business coach you'll ever have.

There's something about those early days—the ones that feel like standing on a wind-swept mountaintop with no shelter in sight. You're exposed, cold, and questioning why on earth you thought this path was a good idea. That's what building something from scratch often feels like. Brutal. Honest. And completely necessary.

When I speak to rooms full of entrepreneurs, dreamers, and doers, I love to ask a straightforward question: *What was the worst day of your work life?*

The room always shifts. People sit straighter or look down at their laps. And then the stories pour in—from the brave ones, at least.

Someone will talk about being fired without warning. Another shares how their work was stolen and presented as someone else's masterpiece. Someone else recalls the sting of being passed over for a promotion they'd worked their soul into. Each tale, a little scar they've carried in silence, now spoken aloud.

Sometimes, yes, these things happen for no good reason. And injustice in the workplace is real. But often, underneath the pain, there's a deeper invitation. One to reflect. To ask: What could I have done differently? What can I learn?

We don't build muscle by skipping the gym. Growth—real, lasting, internal growth—happens under pressure.

I remember a chapter from my own life that I now see as foundational, though at the time it felt like barely surviving. I had taken a job—any job—because I needed to eat. It was in a tech-heavy retail store, selling what was, at the time, the newest novelty: cellular phones. I was young, shy, and painfully awkward. The thought of making conversation with strangers made my skin crawl. But bills don't wait for confidence. Rent doesn't care about your anxiety. And commissions sure as hell don't earn themselves.

I still remember the voice in my head after day one: What have I done?

But I went back. Because I had to. And day by day, awkward conversation by awkward conversation, I started to change. I learned to speak up, to listen, to connect. I learned to sell—but more importantly, I learned to serve. To show up. To grow.

It wasn't glamorous. It was gritty. But it changed my life.

What's even more beautiful? Some of my closest friendships today started in that little retail store. Co-workers, clients, even strangers who trusted me enough to let me help them—they became part of my story. My real network. The kind you don't build in curated boardrooms or exclusive masterminds, but through shared sweat and laughter and long days on your feet.

Here's the truth I hold tight:
Being hungry—literally or metaphorically—is one of the best motivators. Sometimes to eat, you've got to change your game plan. You've got to stretch. You've got to climb. And you've got to talk to people, even when your voice shakes.

And yes, I like to eat. Starving isn't an option.

So, when the winds howl and the mountain feels too steep, remember: those aren't signs to quit. They're signs you're being tempered into someone stronger, someone who can handle the summit you're climbing toward.

Lean in. Keep going. The view is worth it.

***

A Love Letter to the Brave Woman Starting Her Business

For most of my life, I've been a worrier. Not the kind of light, fleeting worry that passes with a sigh—but the deep, preemptive kind. The kind that scripts conversations days before they happen. That builds backup plans for every backup plan. The kind that has me carrying more insurance policies than anyone reasonably should.

It's how I've coped. It's how I've tried to protect the people I love. And maybe, it's how I've tried to protect myself—from disappointment, from failure, from the unknown.

But here's what I've learned the hard way: Worry, when overfed, will rob you of everything beautiful about this moment. It'll cloud the tiny miracles, the quiet victories, the unexpected peace that lives in the in-between spaces of your becoming.

So, if you're reading this, and you've chosen to leap—into entrepreneurship, into something that scares you as much as it thrills you—please stop for just a moment.

Acknowledge your courage.

This decision, this calling, this wild, audacious idea you're holding in your heart… it's not small. Most people never even get this far. They think about it. Dream about it. Talk circles around it. But you? You're doing it. You're here, beginning.

If there's no one nearby to celebrate you, then let me say it now: I am proud of you. Deeply. Wholeheartedly. Without reservation.

And if you need to hear it again tomorrow morning, find the closest mirror and say it to yourself. Yes, even if it feels ridiculous. Give yourself that nod of respect, that

Mel Robbins-style high-five. Or just a small smile that says, *you're showing up*. And that's everything.

The road ahead? It won't be smooth. You will doubt yourself. You'll have nights where you stare at the ceiling, wondering if you've made a huge mistake. There will be financial stress. There will be criticism. There will be moments when you feel entirely alone.

But there will also be breakthroughs. There will be days when a single client email will remind you why you started. There will be tiny victories—your first sale, your first thank-you note, your first moment of realizing, *Gracious! This might actually work.*

And then one day, long after the dust of your first few months has settled, you'll look back and realize: You didn't just survive—you built something.

So, here's what sits deep in my chest:

Don't stop before you even start.
Don't let fear get the final word.
Don't let worry mute your brilliance.

Now is the time to dream, yes—but also to act. To trust your gut, your grit, your grace. To know that you are exactly where you need to be, even in uncertainty.

The world needs what you have to offer. Your voice. Your story. Your light. This isn't just about building a business. It's about building a life—your life—on your terms.

So, take a deep breath.
Ground yourself.
Keep moving.

And whatever you do, don't miss the gifts. Oh, my friend, there are so many gifts.

You've got this. And I am rooting for you, fiercely, every step of the way.

Do not despise these small beginnings, for the Lord rejoices to see the work begin.

-Zacheriah 4:10

***

It started with the most ordinary thing in the world—my ringing cell phone. The sharp trill broke the hush of a late afternoon, eyeball-deep in Human Resources Management exam prep. I welcomed the interruption like a swimmer gasping for air between laps.

"Ashley Burnette," I answered, trying to sound more awake than I felt.

The voice on the other end was strong, assured. It filled the space between my ears with authority. "Hi Ashley, you don't know me, but I'm sitting here looking at your resume, and we need to talk."

For a moment, everything else faded—textbooks, flashcards, even the hum of my laptop. His voice was firm but distant, like it was traveling through fog, and suddenly, the room felt unfamiliar. The air shifted. I stood up, not because I needed to, but because something in me did.

"Executive Director?" I echoed, my voice a mix of confusion and awe.

"Yes," he replied without hesitation, grounding me back into the moment. "Your resume is extremely impressive, and I'd like to discuss a position with you."

In the space of a heartbeat, my brain spun through a mental Rolodex of questions. I hadn't applied for anything recently. Especially not to a nonprofit. Executive Director? That's the kind of title that wears a crown of responsibility, a weighty blend of leadership, pressure, and visibility. And somewhere in that mental scramble: *Who in the world gave him my name?*

"I'm… surprised to hear that," I said, doing my best to keep my voice level. "I'm currently a student, and I run my own business. I'm not quite sure how my resume ended up in your hands."

He paused. The kind of pause that makes you check your phone to see if the call dropped.

Then calmly, as if he knew something I didn't, he said, "Well, sometimes the right people find you, Ashley. I understand if you're not interested, but I'd strongly encourage you to hear us out. I'll email you the job description, and if you'd like to talk further, call me."

Click. Just like that, the call ended.

And just like that, life offered me a curveball I never saw coming.

I sat back down on the soft, aging sofa at the far end of my room, staring at my phone like it had just transformed into a frog turned full-on prince. My laptop screen had gone dark, my neglected study guide now irrelevant. I was nowhere near Human Resources anymore. My mind had bolted straight past the textbook pages and into a realm of possibility I hadn't even dared to imagine.

Surely, I told myself, this was some kind of mix-up. I would politely decline. I'd explain the confusion, and the universe would go back to running on logic. That was the plan.

But then I opened the email.

The subject line was simple. The attachment was ominously titled "Executive Director – Position Description." I clicked. I read. And then my stomach dropped.

Because it wasn't a mix-up. It wasn't a mistake.

Every bullet point on that page—the qualifications, the responsibilities, the vision—fit me. It was me. My past experiences, my odd mix of skills, my values. Somehow, someone had seen me. Not just my résumé, but the rhythm of my work, the weight of my heart.

That was the moment I realized: Sometimes, doors don't wait for you to knock. Sometimes, they swing open with the wind, and that's a complete God thing.

The only thing left for you to do in such moments is decide whether to walk through.

So, to the woman reading this who feels unsure, underqualified, or not-quite-ready: life might be preparing to offer you something you didn't plan for—but something that will fit you like it was sewn to your soul. Don't dismiss it. Don't back away out of fear.

Sometimes, the path to purpose doesn't come with a grand introduction. Sometimes, it just rings your phone.

Pick up.

Let's talk for a few minutes about being ready for unexpected opportunities.

Success isn't always about the hustle. It's not always found in the relentless chase or the non-stop networking or the next big opportunity you're trying to wrangle into submission. Sometimes—maybe even most of the time—success shows up quietly, and only when you're ready to receive it.

It's about being steady. Being faithful. Being prepared—not just for what you want, but for what you didn't even know was coming.

And sometimes? You just need to be still.
(Be still and know that I am God. Psalm 46:10.) It is not

an easy verse to follow, but it has served me well more times than I can count.

I wasn't looking for that role. My hands were already full—business showing the first modest signs of bloom, school in session, life moving faster than I could keep up with. I had my eyes locked on a completely different horizon.

But my résumé and my reputation—those spoke for me when I didn't even know there was a room they needed to enter. More importantly, God spoke for me. He knew what I didn't: *that just around the bend was a season I wouldn't be able to navigate alone.* A stretch of road where I'd need real support. The kind that holds your arms up when you're too tired to lift them yourself.

So, He made space. A place of honor, wrapped in grace, among people who loved Him—and in time, came to love and champion me, too.

This season taught me something unexpected: Excellence matters, even when no one's watching. Especially then.

I wasn't trying to build a personal brand. I wasn't out here curating a platform. I was just showing up. Doing the work. Treating people with kindness, even on the days it felt like I had nothing left to give. That quiet consistency? It wasn't glamorous. But it was growing something beneath the surface. Something real. Something lasting.

Back when I was stuck in that clinic where I started— miserable, overlooked, eventually dismissed without so much as a thank-you—I couldn't see it. I couldn't see how any of it could possibly be part of something good.

But the seeds I'd sown? They had taken root.

That's the thing about faithfulness in hard seasons. It plants the kind of fruit that finds its way back to you. It circles around in the form of divine timing. In whispers you almost miss. In phone calls that change everything. In doors that open not because you knocked, but because you lived in a way that made the opening inevitable.

So, if you're in a quiet season right now, where the work feels thankless and the vision feels somehow too remote, don't stop. Keep tending. Keep showing up. Keep doing good work, not because you're being watched, but because it's who you are.

The reward? It may not come fast. But it will come full and right on time.

You're probably wondering how that phone call even came to be. Honestly? So was I.

It started with a whisper—an almost forgettable moment tucked inside a short freelance gig for a business owner I barely knew. I had worked hard, kept my head down, delivered what I promised. We didn't share late-night strategy calls or long lunches. Just a handful of emails and a mutual respect for getting things done.

What I didn't know then—what still humbles me now— is that she saw something in my work. Enough to mention my name, not to a recruiter, not even to someone in her own company, but to her husband. Her husband. Who happened to sit on the board of a small but mighty clinic. He passed my résumé along to the board president. And by that evening, I got a phone call that would change the course of my career.

Let that sink in: someone spoke my name in a room I didn't even know existed.

That moment taught me something I carry with me to this day—something I want you to carry too, especially if you're building from the ground up or trying to pivot into the version of your business you know it's meant to be.

Your *name* can go places long before you ever set foot in the room.

And that's why this part of the journey—your relationships, your effort, your reputation—matters more than you might think. People will talk about you when you're not around. For the love of all that is good and true, give them something kind, something powerful, something undeniable to say.

So how do you do that?

You show up. Not just when it's convenient or glamorous, but when it's hard and quiet and you think no one's watching. You show up then. You deliver. Not just the bare minimum, but with excellence that echoes. You build real, honest connections with the people around you—not as steppingstones, but as fellow travelers. You treat your network not as a ladder to climb, but as a community to nourish.

You do the work. And you do it with integrity that doesn't buckle under pressure.

Because here's the truth: you never know which small project, which passing conversation, which moment of excellence will become the spark that lights your next path.

I didn't see that phone call coming. I didn't orchestrate it. But I did plant the seeds.

And sister, so can you.

Impostor syndrome—the fear that once people really see you, they'll wonder how you ever got through the door—is a quiet thief. It doesn't kick the door down. It seeps in through the cracks, whispering that you're not enough, that it's only a matter of time before someone calls you out.

And let me tell you, when the opportunity in front of you is bigger than anything you've ever dared to reach for, that whisper becomes a roar.

Did I doubt myself when I was offered the role? Without question. But if you've walked with me this far, you probably already guessed that.

What I was still untangling then—what I hadn't fully healed from—wasn't just professional. It was personal. I was carrying the weight of a former leader who had no interest in seeing me rise. A woman who made it painfully clear I wasn't welcome in her orbit, let alone under her mentorship. She gave me no development, no encouragement, no space to grow. Just silence. And for a while, I mistook that silence for truth. I let it echo every doubt I'd been rehearsing since girlhood.

Because long before the workplace, I had been taught—indirectly, quietly, cruelly—that belonging had to be earned through perfection. That vulnerability was dangerous. That I could be loved only if I performed just right.

I learned that in classrooms where I shrank my curiosity to fit in. I learned it in friendships that faltered the moment I needed more than I gave. And I learned it, slowly and heartbreakingly, in a marriage where I lost myself trying to keep peace that never truly existed.

So yeah, by the time that job offer came in, I was already carrying layers of self-doubt like old coats I hadn't figured out how to shed.

But here's the thing.

What I didn't realize—what so many of us don't—is that the preparation was already happening. Not in grand stages or applause-filled moments, but in the quiet work. The resilience. The long days when I showed up, even when I didn't feel seen. The skills I built. The persistence that didn't shout but never quit.

The role I was offered? It didn't ask me to become someone new. It recognized who I already was.

Fear is just the static trying to keep you from tuning into your purpose. Don't let it win.

God didn't bring you this far to leave you gasping for air. He's not careless. He's not random. He is a master of timing, and grace, and redemption.

That unexpected call? It disrupted everything I thought I was building. But it also handed me something that had once felt out of reach. And receiving it didn't require more pain, more proving, or more perfection. It just required me to be open. To pivot. To believe, maybe for the first time in a long time, that what was being offered wasn't a fluke.

It was already mine.

Preparation. Education. Experience. Skill. These weren't random threads. They were stitches in a tapestry I hadn't fully seen yet. And then one day, they aligned—clicked into place—and set me in front of a door I hadn't even dared to ask for. But here's the beautiful truth: I wasn't surprised by the door. I was ready for it.

It wasn't luck. It wasn't a favor or a fluke. It was alignment. A divine culmination of years spent laboring in quiet corners, of saying yes to growth when no one was applauding. A moment of grace where everything I had poured out in silence met the timing only God could orchestrate.

Thank You, Father.

We talk so much about being ready when opportunity knocks. But what we don't say enough is that readiness is slow. It's built in the mundane: In the study that no one sees. In the late-night note-taking. In the early-morning emails. In the days when you're showing up to a dream that still looks more like a whisper than a reality.

I learned that during the aching, silent years of my adolescence—when my voice felt too small and my ambitions too much. I learned it in a marriage where I kept showing up, hoping love would meet me halfway, only to realize that sometimes growth comes through grief.

And yet—through every disappointment, every lesson, every "not yet"—I was becoming. Not just professionally. Personally. Spiritually. Emotionally. I was becoming someone who could carry more, love better, lead more deeply.

That's the thing about preparation. It often feels like nothing's happening. Like you're stuck in place while everyone else is sprinting ahead. But under the surface, roots are growing. Muscles are forming. Vision is sharpening.

So, if you're in a season where it feels like you're grinding for a goal that no one else can see—keep going. Keep learning. Keep growing. Keep showing up for the vision that's been placed on your heart, even when it feels fragile.

Because even when it seems like nothing's moving, something is.

And when the moment finally arrives—when that door swings open—it won't feel foreign or too big. It'll feel like home. Like it was waiting for you.

Not because you stumbled into it by chance. But because you were becoming it all along.

He called out of the blue—this man who would one day become my boss—and said he'd stumbled across an old version of my résumé. Outdated, imperfect, a little rough around the edges. I remember wincing when he mentioned it, already rehearsing all the ways I'd explain the gaps and the growth since then.

But he didn't ask for any explanations.

He saw something in me I hadn't yet dared to see in myself. Not who I was on paper, but who I could be. He believed in a future version of me—still in the making, still unfolding.

And sometimes? That's what it takes. To borrow someone else's belief until our own gets strong enough to stand on its own.

Think about that. When someone sees potential in you— when they offer you a chance, a seat at the table, a stretch assignment that makes your stomach flip—pause before you dismiss it. Ask yourself: What are they seeing that I've been too scared or too modest to claim?

Maybe, just maybe, they're not wrong.

Maybe they're catching a glimpse of a strength you haven't named yet, a flicker of brilliance you've been keeping under wraps, waiting until you feel "ready."

But readiness is overrated. Most of the big, beautiful leaps in life aren't about being ready—they're about being willing. Willing to show up. Willing to grow.

Willing to let it be messy and magical and full of becoming.

Because more often than not, that belief someone else placed in you? It wasn't misplaced.

It was just early.

During my time as a single parent, I found myself in the trenches with others who knew exactly what that life felt like. We bonded over cold cups of coffee and half-eaten meals, exchanging the silent understanding that comes from holding everything together with duct tape and prayers. Some of us had a little more help, some a little less—but we all carried that familiar ache of trying to do it all, often feeling like we were coming up short.

One acquaintance was a man named Gary, a father raising two teenage daughters on his own after losing his wife. His quiet strength humbled me. One evening, surrounded by a few friends, I started to spill over. The weight of it all came tumbling out—how I couldn't afford my son's class ring, how I didn't know if we'd still have health insurance next month. It wasn't just the money. It was the constant pressure, the fear, the never-ending list of things I couldn't seem to fix.

Gary didn't interrupt, and everyone at the table kept quiet, too. Then, he just looked me straight in the eye and said, "Eat the damn elephant."

I blinked. *What?* I'd never heard the phrase before. He saw my confusion and gently explained: "When you have to eat an elephant, you do it one bite at a time."

It stuck with me. Because that's exactly what life felt like—like trying to swallow something impossibly large. But Gary's words gave me a starting point. They gave me permission to stop expecting myself to fix everything at once. One bite. One small action. One choice to move forward instead of staying stuck.

And that lesson? It didn't just carry me through those long parenting nights or the terrifying months of uncertainty—it's followed me into every intimidating moment since. Like the time an opportunity came my way that felt "too right," so much so that I almost turned it down out of fear. Not because it wasn't a perfect fit, but because it scared the hell out of me. The alignment was too good, too clear—and that kind of clarity can be its own kind of terrifying.

Big opportunities often are. They demand more of us. They ask us to stretch, to grow, to shed the familiar and step into the uncharted. But growth doesn't happen in still water. It happens when we move. When we risk. When we say yes even when our hands are shaking.

So, if you're staring at something that feels impossibly large right now—whether it's a job, a bill, a broken relationship, or a dream so big it makes your throat tighten—start with one bite. Write the email. Make the call. Ask the question. Say yes, even if you don't feel ready.

Because readiness is a myth. Willingness is where the magic is.

And once you learn how to eat the elephant, no challenge will ever look the same again. You'll see obstacles not as roadblocks, but as meals to be taken one bite at a time. You'll show up stronger. Wiser. More capable than you ever thought you could be.

So go on. Take the bite.

My mother was a prayer warrior of the fiercest kind. The kind who met every crossroads—every heartbreak, every hard yes or impossible no—on her knees. Her prayer didn't shift much, but it didn't need to. "God, please open the right doors and close the wrong ones." That was her refrain. Simple. Steady. Sure.

It's the prayer I whisper to myself now, quietly, when I'm standing at the edge of a big decision. When clarity is a stranger and the stakes feel like they couldn't be higher. As a mother, I whisper it when I'm worried I'm not getting it right. As a business leader, when I'm making a call that will ripple through other people's lives. As a wife in a second marriage that I cherish more than words can hold, I whisper it when I want to show up in love, not fear. And in the moments when I'm simply trying to be a good neighbor, a present friend, a steady force in a world that shifts by the hour—I return to it.

Because here's what I've come to believe: faith is not the absence of fear. It's what you reach for when fear is loud and heavy and convincing. Faith is your protection. Your armor. Your peace. But it's also your biggest asset— your inner compass that keeps you moving when everything in you wants to stay still.

Not every door is meant to open. Not every plan will unfold the way you pictured it. (Thank God for that, by the way. Some of the most painful closed doors were also the ones that saved me.) Some of the strangest turns brought me to the most meaningful places. And more than once, I've found myself grateful for the "no" that made space for a better "yes."

So, if you're staring down a decision right now—if life feels tangled and uncertain—I want you to know this: you don't have to know all the answers. You just have to know where your trust lies. You just have to listen for that stirring in your spirit. Because when something scares you and speaks to you? When it stretches your comfort but tugs at your purpose? That's holy ground.

Be ready to walk through the right doors. Be willing to let go of the ones that close. And don't fear the dark hallways in between. That's where faith grows legs. That's where you build the resilience you'll need—not just for the next step, but for the life you're being called to live.

It won't always look like what you imagined. But if you keep choosing courage over comfort, faith over fear—I promise, it will shape you into someone who can handle what's waiting on the other side.

And maybe one day, someone will say the same thing about you that I say about my mother: She met every crossroads on her knees. And she never once stood alone.

My grace is sufficient for you; My power is made perfect in weakness.

-2 Corinthians 12:9

Chapter 6

Finding Purpose in the Hard Seasons

My world looked completely different just a few months after that life-altering phone call. Suddenly, I was a small business owner and the only full-time employee at a small Christian clinic—an hour-long commute each way, multiple times a week. I wore a lot of hats. At one job, I brainstormed with creatives who made magic from scratch; at the other, I served alongside volunteers whose hearts were lit with purpose and compassion. It was full and demanding—and it was beautiful. Each morning, I woke up tired but grateful. I saw God's fingerprints in every conversation, every spreadsheet, every moment of chaos.

Life was shifting in other places too. After years of weathering life alone, I married Adam Davis—a good man in every sense. Steady, kind, handsome in that rugged, real-life way that doesn't need announcing. He didn't try to fix me. He held space. He showed up. Adam is the kind of man who meets life head-on, with quiet strength and rolled-up sleeves. And in marrying him, I didn't just gain a partner—I gained a reminder that good love builds.

Meanwhile, my son was beginning the harrowing process of applying to military academies. That alone would keep any mother up at night. And my little business? It was inching forward—sometimes leaping with excitement, other times bumbling like a toddler learning to walk. Life felt like it was moving at lightning speed, and I was clinging to the ride, doing my best not to fall off.

Then came another call. Another open door. This time, it was home calling— a non-profit that was all about the development of Downtown Sevierville, Tennessee. They wanted me to become the Main Street Director, overseeing events, small business development, and a major historic renovation project at the county's Heritage Museum. The museum lived inside a 1940s WPA Post Office and needed a full resurrection. Fundraising, grants, meetings with county officials—the whole nine yards. It was the kind of dream a nerdy, history-loving girl like me had tucked away in her back pocket for years.

I should have hesitated.

I didn't.

"When can I start?" I said.

The days that followed were anything but easy. I was now balancing three distinct businesses—two of them nonprofits that required not just strategy but heart. These weren't places where success was measured in likes or ad impressions. These were places where impact meant lives changed, hope renewed. And behind it all was a marriage I wanted to get right this time. A son I wanted to support through one of the hardest challenges a young man can face. And a God I was learning to trust in ways I never had before.

It was exhausting. It was overwhelming. And, of course, rife with lessons.

There were late nights where my to-do list haunted me. Mornings that started before the sun and stretched long past what was reasonable. And in the middle of it all, I prayed. A lot. Sometimes desperate, sometimes determined, always honest. "Lord, I need you in this." And every time, He showed up—in rescheduled meetings, in a friend's unexpected encouragement, in a strength that didn't feel like mine.

Here's what I've learned: God never wastes the hard seasons. He's not in the business of burning us out for fun. He's in the business of building capacity. Expanding faith. Teaching us how to rise when the world insists we should fall. And most importantly—He reminds us we were never meant to do it alone.

If you're in a hard season right now—if you're juggling dreams and deadlines, love and loss, ambition and exhaustion—hear me: you are not crazy, and you are not alone.

The work you're doing matters. And the weariness you feel? It's evidence that you're showing up in all the ways that count. If God has placed something in your hands—an idea, a business, a calling, a person to love—He's not setting you up to fail. He's equipping you to carry it.

So no, you don't have to do it perfectly. You just have to do it faithfully. Keep showing up. Keep saying yes.

Because finding purpose isn't about sitting on a couch waiting for clarity. It's about getting up, stepping in, doing the work—even when it's messy, even when it's maddening. Especially when it's hard.

And if you're lucky—really lucky—you'll have someone standing beside you, a friend, a mentor, a spouse. Not to save you. Not to solve it. But to believe in you. To lift what they can. To love you steadily. I believe God gives us people. I will keep saying it: Make sure to look for yours.

Also, roll up your sleeves, friend.

Let's talk about what it really means to build something that matters.

When you're stretched too thin—and trust me, you will be—your first instinct will be to tell yourself that you're not enough. You will repeat that there is not enough time, not enough energy, not enough know-how to keep up with everything suddenly flying at you like a storm. It'll feel like you're failing simply because you're overwhelmed. But I want to gently challenge that narrative.

Capacity isn't some tool you can pick up in the checkout line at Target after a long day. It's not instant. It's not easy. It's earned. Grown. Built one hard, holy moment at a time.

If this is your first business, your first leadership role, your first time trying to carry the weight of a dream and a family and your faith and your own aching soul—all while trying not to drop any of it—you're not supposed to know how to do it all. Not yet. Maybe not ever perfectly. You learn while you're in the thick of it, shoulder-deep in the mess and the magic of building something real.

You learn in the trenches.

And yes, it will feel like a grind. A gut-punch. Some days, it will feel like everything is too much. (My son, with his military wisdom, calls this "embracing the suck." A brutal but honest way of saying: lean in anyway.)

You'll grow in the moments when you're tempted to give up, but don't. When you pause to pray through the tears, when you decide to trust that the process isn't just shaping your business—it's shaping you. When you dare to believe that discomfort isn't a detour, it's the training ground.

This season won't last forever. But the person you become in it? That strength, that grit, that grace under pressure—that's yours to keep.

So don't run from the hard. Meet it. Face it. Grow through it.

As a military mama, I have heard repeatedly that soldiers must learn not how to juggle all the balls that are thrown at them, but to learn which ones are rubber and which ones are glass. It's something we all need to learn to move forward effectively.

When in doubt, remember you're not failing. You're being forged.

When that invitation came to step into the role of Main Street Director, it didn't land in an empty season. My hands were already full; I was juggling balls like a madwoman. My calendar was packed and my soul was forging through battles that don't show up on a normal to-do list. The logical, self-protective part of me had every reason to say no. To guard my peace. To stay in my lane. To not tip the scales any further in a life already stretched at the seams.

But life—real, growth-fueled life—rarely waits for our calendars to clear or for everything to line up just right.

Growth doesn't knock politely. It crashes in. It interrupts. It invites us to rise when we feel like we're already falling. It says, "Now is the time," even when we whisper back, "But I'm not ready."

I've learned that saying yes doesn't always feel brave at first. Sometimes it feels shaky. Sometimes it feels foolish. Sometimes your voice cracks when you speak the words aloud. But trembling doesn't mean unqualified. It means human.

Here's what anchors me: God doesn't always call the ones with the most experience or the most free time or the neatest lives. He calls those willing to walk forward, even when the path is foggy. And then—*then*—He equips them in the going. He qualifies the called, not vice versa.

So, if the door opens—if it stirs something in your spirit, if it whispers to a purpose planted deep in your bones—

don't let fear be the loudest voice in the room. Don't wait for everything to feel "right."

Walk through it anyway. Walk through it messy. Walk through it scared. Walk through it feeling wildly unprepared. And trust that on the other side of that door, grace will be waiting with arms full of what you didn't know you'd need.

Because sometimes, the most sacred growth comes not in waiting for the moment, but in choosing to believe you were made for it—even if your knees shake while you step forward.

One of the hardest, most humbling lessons I've had to learn as an entrepreneur is this: you might start alone, but you cannot grow alone.

And if you're someone who's spent years pushing through with grit and sheer willpower—balancing vision with survival—it's a lesson that can feel almost like betrayal. Because at the beginning, it was all you. Your late nights. Your name on the dotted line. Your dreams sketched out in journals and prayed over in quiet moments when no one else could see.

When the business feels like your baby, releasing control feels a lot like letting go of a limb. You want to protect it. You want to do it right. And sometimes that means clinging too tightly—until your own hands become the very thing suffocating the dream.

Because here's what happens if you try to carry it all alone: you hit the wall. Not a wall. *The wall*. The one that doesn't budge no matter how hard you hustle. The one that says, "You've maxed out. It's time to stop pretending you can do it all."

The moment of truth came for me when a friend and client walked through my door and asked me if I was okay. I verbally vomited the absolute truth: I was drowning. I didn't know how I was going to survive, to get things done, to keep from disappointing the people who had hired me. He didn't say much, and he left the office. I was certain he thought I'd had a mental break.

Two hours later, his wife showed up and simply asked, "What do you need me to do?" and just like that, I had an employee.

For me, breaking through that wall meant learning to hire. Learning to outsource. Learning to delegate with trust, not just instruction. It meant loosening my grip— not out of apathy, but out of fierce love for what I'm building. Because I care enough to know I can't carry this alone.

A one-woman show is impressive…until the lights burn out and there's no one left to pull the curtain back up.

So, I started to build a cast. A crew. A team. Not just anyone, but people who saw what I saw—and even more importantly, people who could see what I didn't. People who brought their own gifts to the table and made the dream bigger, stronger, more sustainable.

And I won't pretend it's easy. Trusting others with pieces of your vision is vulnerable work. But it's also necessary. Because at some point, the measure of your leadership stops being what you can do alone—and starts being what you can build together.

So, if you're standing at that wall right now, exhausted and unsure how to scale it, this is your sign: you need people. Good people. Brave people. People who will help you carry the weight, brick by brick.

Trust them. Trust the process. And trust that your dream—your baby—will grow healthier and more beautiful when you stop trying to do it all alone.

Another thing I've learned from running multiple businesses is this: structure isn't a luxury.

It's survival.

Now, I don't say that as someone who was born organized or thrives in a world of perfectly color-coded calendars. I say it as a wildly creative soul—a big-picture thinker with mismatched socks, notebooks full of half-sketched dreams, and a mind that never really powers down. I am, at my core, more spark than system. But that spark? It burns out fast without something steady to hold it.

At first, I resisted the structure. Thought it might box me in or dim the fire. Systems, workflows, boundaries— they felt cold and corporate. Foreign to someone who'd rather create than calculate. But burnout has a way of teaching you what busy never will: without boundaries, everything breaks. Including you.

What I've come to understand—deep in my bones—is that structure isn't the enemy of creativity. It's the bodyguard.

Clear workflows. Automated tasks. Boundaries that aren't just written down but actually honored. These aren't just productivity hacks. They are the scaffolding that holds up your dream when your energy, time, or brain space runs thin.

I once heard that Mark Zuckerberg wore the same hoodie and jeans every day while building Facebook—not because he lacked style, but because it was one less decision to make. One tiny system that carved out more space for what actually mattered. That kind of simplicity? That's not lazy. That's strategic. That's wise.

Because here's the truth: whether you're managing a team or managing your own beautiful chaos, you need rhythms. You need structure that lets you breathe, not just hustle. Systems that help you stay anchored when the winds of entrepreneurship threaten to toss you around.

It's not about becoming rigid. It's about becoming rooted.

Because structure doesn't stifle your creativity—it protects it. It gives your ideas a place to land, your energy a place to recharge, and your vision a fighting chance to grow.

So, if you're drowning in good intentions and unfinished projects, it might be time to build some scaffolding, by hiring people who are good with systems and data if that's not your thing, or who are creative thinkers if you aren't. Not because you're failing. But because you finally understand what it takes to sustain the fire– some diversity of thought. A pair of good minds is better than one, and a group is better than a pair. The more differently you think than the people you surround yourself with, the more great ideas and structure will fall into place. This is a good thing. Allow it to happen.

You can't separate faith and business.

I pray over my office almost every morning before the doors open. Some days it's a quick breath of gratitude, other days it's a plea for peace, for clarity, for provision. I pray over my team. I pray over our payroll. I pray when there's tension in the room, and I pray when we're laughing so hard we can barely get any work done. I pray for our clients—even the difficult ones. Especially the difficult ones. I ask that we serve them well, or, if we're not the right fit, that the parting would be swift, gentle, and filled with grace.

I don't know how many people pray over their businesses like this. I can't speak for anyone else. I just know that I do.

Because I can't separate my faith from any other part of my life. And business? Business is where it shows up the most for me nowadays.

Faith and business aren't two separate lanes for me— they're woven together. Not in theory, not in metaphor, but in the gritty, everyday reality of showing up and leading something that matters. People often try to keep faith tidy and business strategic, as if they are puzzle pieces that don't quite fit. But in the real world, they bleed together. They must.

Every hard decision I've faced—every time I've wondered whether to hire, to let go, to stretch the budget, to walk away from a shiny opportunity that didn't sit right in my spirit—those weren't just business calls. They were faith calls. They were answered in prayer, made possible by trust, and often walked out on shaking legs.

Once, we had a major client lined up—a big one, the kind of contract that could've changed the financial landscape of our year. Everything looked good on paper. But my spirit was uneasy. I prayed, hard. For days. Then I called a meeting, asked a few questions, and the mask fell away. The deal wasn't right. We walked away, and I exhaled a quiet "thank you" to a God who saw what I couldn't.

Faith shaped that moment. Not strategy. Not profit margins. Today, I am grateful.

This is the stuff that can't be tracked in metrics or mapped on a quarterly review. But it's real. It's why I open every month with prayer. It's why I pause in the middle of a heated email draft to ask for grace. It's why I pray over my team even on the days I feel empty.

Because the truth is, God doesn't just meet me in my quiet time or on Sunday morning. He meets me in the pitch meeting. In the conference call. In the chaos of deadlines and decisions. He's in the spreadsheet. The sticky notes. The sacred and the seemingly small.

Let Him in.

Not just into your hopes, but into your plans. Not just into your heart, but into your hiring practices. Invite Him into your branding, your client calls, your quarterly goals. Let Him walk the office floor with you. Let Him sit in on the meetings. Invite Him into every part of the dream you're building.

Because when faith and business move together—when they are not just co-existing but co-creating—something shifts.

It stops being about what you can build. And starts being about what God can build through you.

Let your light shine before others, that they may see your good deeds and glorify your Father in heaven

-Matthew 5:16

You can't connect the dots looking forward; you can only connect them looking backward. -Steve Jobs

Chapter 7

Things No One Told Me About Business

There are certain things about business that I wish I had known sooner. Warning: This may be the most dry chapter of this book, and yet, it's the most necessary. Dreams may be born in the quiet corners of your heart, but businesses are built in the grit of the everyday—budget spreadsheets, client calls, contracts, and the oh-so-glamorous world of QuickBooks reconciliation. You're going to learn quickly that passion alone won't keep the lights on. You need skills. Systems. Strategies. The things nobody posts about on Instagram because they're not cute, and they don't come with a filter.

If you are creative, you need to hold on to this. This is the part that matters. This is the scaffolding that holds the dream steady.

Below are the things I had to learn the hard way. I hope with everything in me, these insights provide you the ability to dodge a few bullets along your journey. The best of us learn from the mistakes of others, so I am outing myself. Here's what haunted me in the dark—things I got dead wrong, lost sleep over, and would go back and redo in a heartbeat if I could.

Now, marketing has been my wheelhouse for a long time, but it isn't everyone's, so here's a starter kit for doing it well:

If your business were a body, marketing would be its circulation system—the thing moving oxygen (your message) to the places where life can grow. You cannot ignore it, and you cannot "do it later." Marketing is not optional. It *is* the work. I know this must sound rich coming from me, a marketer, but my stomach really does sink when people don't get marketing right. It can make or break your business. If you aren't a subject matter expert, you need one in your corner. And yes, there are shady people in this industry, so choose wisely.

This is what I wish I'd understood that people need to know about marketing:

Your Message Matters More Than Your Polish

Let's get one thing straight: people don't buy because your branding photos look like a magazine spread. They buy because they *trust* you. If your marketing agency is more concerned with cashing your check than amplifying your voice, it's time to walk away. You need someone who listens to your story, understands what you're about, and can help you share that message in a way that resonates—deeply and honestly.

Too many businesses settle for campaigns that "sound good" but say nothing real. If someone's just crafting a pitch that looks good on paper but feels hollow, your audience will feel that disconnect and quietly disappear. People know when they're being sold to—and nobody likes it. But everyone wants a problem solved. If your marketing speaks to their *real need,* and offers a clear, human solution, they will lean in.

Your business shouldn't feel like a sales trap—it should feel like a *helping hand.* Your messaging is what makes that happen. Prioritize truth over polish. Always.

Consistency Beats Intensity

You don't need to be everywhere, every day. What you need is to be *recognizable* and *reliable.* Show up consistently—on social media, in your emails, in your community—and do it with purpose. True marketing success isn't about going viral. It's about building a brand that people know, trust, and return to.

Think of it like this: when someone sees your logo, they should feel something. Familiarity. Trust. Comfort. That kind of emotional connection doesn't happen in a week. It's built over time, with every post, every piece of packaging, every voicemail or follow-up. Every interaction is a tiny thread in the larger fabric of your brand.

Not every interaction is a sale, and that's okay. You're not trying to make a sale every time—you're trying to make a connection. Do that often enough, and the sales will come.

You're not just building revenue—you're building *reputation.* That's what lasts.

Marketing Is Storytelling

This one's close to my heart. People don't care about what you do until they understand *why it matters to them.* Don't list your services. Don't rattle off your features. Tell me how my life gets better if I choose you.

Let's say you run a women's clothing boutique. You could say:

"We sell affordable fashion and accessories for everyday wear."

Okay. Technically true. But does it light a fire? Does it stop someone scrolling on their phone or walking down Main Street?

Now try this:

"I help women walk into their closets and smile again. We sell clothes that fit real bodies and real lives—no weird sizing, no snobby sales floor. Just style that feels like *you.*"

That version speaks to *how someone feels* after interacting with your business. That's marketing. That's what people remember. That's what makes them come back.

Your story—and how you tell it—*is* your marketing.

Video Builds Trust Faster Than Anything Else

I know, I know—no one likes seeing themselves on camera. But hear me out: people connect with people. They don't just want to see your product; they want to see *you.*

Video helps your audience get a sense of your tone, your body language, your heart. And in a world that scrolls fast and reads slow, video gives them a reason to stop and listen. You don't have to be polished. You don't need a ring light or a script. Just tell the truth. Tell a story. Share a quick tip. Be real.

Even if your voice shakes, show up anyway. Even if you're nervous, do it anyway. Because someone out there is waiting to hear from someone *like you*— someone they can trust.

Ask for Referrals—Every Time

Here's the part nobody tells you when you start a business: people want to help. They just don't always know *how*—until you ask.

And no, I'm not talking about begging or awkward sales scripts. I'm talking about honesty. The kind that makes people nod and say, "Sure, I can do that."

Say something like:

"Hey, we're trying to get the word out about our new soaps. If you love it, would you tell your friends?"

That's it. No pressure. No guilt. Just a simple ask, rooted in confidence and integrity. And you'd be surprised how many people will follow through.

Sometimes, the best form of marketing is a conversation at a dinner table you're not even at.

Just Show Up Like a Human

Marketing isn't a megaphone. It's a mirror. It reflects what you believe, how you treat people, and how you make their lives better. If you do it with authenticity, consistency, and kindness, the results will come—maybe not instantly, but deeply and sustainably.

So don't overthink the perfect post or the perfect photo. Start by telling the truth. Start by helping someone. Start by being *you.*

Tools That Actually Help:

Marketing doesn't have to break the bank—especially when you're just starting out. There are incredible tools out there that are either free or low-cost, and they can help you look professional, stay consistent, and reach the right people without hiring a full agency. One of the most popular is **Canva**, which is basically graphic design for non-designers. Whether you need a flyer, a social media post, or a professional-looking proposal, Canva has templates that make you look polished without needing a degree in Photoshop. Then there's **Meta Business Suite** (if you're using Facebook or Instagram), which lets you schedule posts ahead of time. This means you can carve out one afternoon a week, plan your content, and then get back to running your business instead of being glued to your phone every day.

For email marketing—which still works better than most people think—**MailChimp** and **Constant Contact** are both user-friendly platforms that help you stay in touch with your audience. Whether you're sending out monthly updates, promo codes, or heartfelt letters to your community, these tools make it easy to connect. When it comes to planning your content (and keeping your head on straight), **Trello** and **Asana** are lifesavers. They help you map out your marketing ideas, organize campaigns, and track tasks—all in one place, so nothing slips through the cracks.

And yes, I'll say it out loud: **ChatGPT** is a game-changer. If writing feels like pulling teeth, this tool can help you draft social posts, brainstorm captions, or polish that email you've been avoiding. It won't replace your voice, but it can help you find it faster. These tools aren't magic, but they are powerful—and most importantly, they put professional-level marketing within reach, even when the budget says otherwise.

Branding

Wait. Didn't we just cover this? No, ma'am. While it's closely tied to marketing, branding is its own beast.

Branding isn't just your color palette, your fonts, or that cute logo you paid someone on **Fiverr** to make. Those things matter—but they're not *the brand.* Branding is the emotional imprint you leave on someone. It's the story that unfolds in their head—and heart—when your business name comes up in conversation. It's whether they feel trust, warmth, relief, respect… or nothing at all.

Think about it like this: when someone hears the name of your business, what do you *want* them to feel? Reassurance? Excitement? Comfort? A sense of being seen? That's your brand. Not the visuals—the *visceral.* For example, if you own a bakery, branding isn't just about having pretty packaging. It's about whether someone walks out with a warm cookie and a warmer heart. If they leave saying, "That place just makes me feel good," *that's branding.*

Your brand lives in the *total experience*: how you answer the phone, how your staff treats customers, what your website says (and how it says it), whether you own your mistakes when something goes wrong. It's how you show up in your community. It's the tone in your emails. It's the vibe in your shop. It's whether people feel invited or dismissed, understood or overlooked.

A beautiful logo might get someone's attention. But your *brand*—the emotional truth of who you are—decides if they'll come back and tell someone else about you. That's the part that can't be faked, rushed, or outsourced. And that's the part people remember.

While beautiful design and polished visuals absolutely help your brand stand out, it's the *message* behind them that moves people. Words and visuals work best *together*, but if you have to choose one to get right first—start with clarity in what you say. A stunning logo won't save a confusing offer. A gorgeous website won't matter if your visitors can't tell what you do within ten seconds. That's why strong copy—your actual *words*—matters so much. It's how you communicate your heart, your offer, and your value.

That said, we also live in a highly visual world. Video builds trust faster than anything else because it combines words *and* presence. Your face, your voice, your body language—they all carry emotional weight that words on a page can't always reach alone. So don't think of copy and visuals as being in competition. Think of them as teammates. Use video to connect. Use words to clarify. Use design to reinforce. The magic happens when all three are working in sync, telling the same story, in your voice.

For instance, if you are a mobile dog groomer, you might say, "We bring the spa to your driveway. Mobile dog grooming that's gentle, convenient, and tailored to your pet. No crates. No chaos. Just clean, happy pups—and a little extra peace of mind for you." While the accompanying visuals show off a clean, playful logo with a bubbly dog silhouette; a consistent color palette (soft blues, warm whites, calming neutrals); Simple, friendly icons for "Nail Trim," "Full Groom," and "Puppy's First Bath;" and before-and-after dog photos with happy client testimonials layered in. (The visuals should be inviting and consistent with the tone of the video and copy—they should feel *gentle, trustworthy,* and *professional,* just like the service itself.)

Ask Yourself:

- What three words describe my business?
- What problem do I solve better than anyone else?
- Would a stranger understand what I offer in 10 seconds?

If the answer is "no," start there.

Budgeting

Listen, I know—it's not fun. But your budget is not a cage; it's a compass. And when you're building from the ground up, you need direction more than ever.

If there's one thing I wish someone had sat me down and told me before I launched my business, it's this: *money will not manage itself*—and if you don't learn to manage it, it will manage *you.* With stress. With sleepless nights. With quiet dread that sneaks up around tax season or when the checking account hits double digits. Most of us didn't start businesses because we love bookkeeping or spreadsheets. We started because we had a dream, a skill, a calling. But none of that matters if the numbers don't work. Passion will get you moving, but discipline is what keeps the lights on.

This chapter isn't about fancy financial strategies or ten-year forecasts. It's about real-life money truths—the kind that keep your doors open and your peace intact. We're going to talk about taxes (sorry), lean operations, break-even points, and the kind of common-sense budgeting advice you can actually use even if math makes your head hurt. It's not glamorous, but it's *essential.* Because the goal isn't just to build a business that inspires people. It's to build one that pays your bills, funds your future, and leaves you room to breathe.

Every Dollar Needs a Job

I'm going to go a little Dave Ramsey here. If you don't assign your money a job, it will wander—and probably end up in a coffee shop, a random subscription, or a fourth trip to Target. In business, money without direction is a slow leak you don't notice until something breaks.

Let's say you make $2,000 in a week from client work. That sounds great—until you realize that $600 of it went to untracked supplies, impulse purchases, and tools you don't even use. You *thought* you were profitable, but your money was freelancing without permission.

Start simple: when income comes in, divide it. A portion for taxes. A portion for operating expenses. A portion to pay yourself. A portion for savings or reinvestment. You don't need fancy software—just a system. Think of your dollars like employees. If they don't have clear roles, they'll waste time, slack off, and create chaos.

Taxes Are Real. And They Hurt.

Let's not sugarcoat it: taxes are a gut-punch if you don't plan for them. One of the hardest lessons many small business owners learn is the feeling of pride turning to panic when tax season hits. That "extra" money you thought you had? Uncle Sam wants his share—and he's not subtle about it.

I've seen too many entrepreneurs crumble under the weight of back taxes they didn't see coming. Don't let that be you. From day one, set aside 25–30% of your net income in a separate account. Every time you get paid. Even if it feels too early. Even if it's "just a little." Because here's the truth: you will *never* miss money you planned to save—but you will definitely miss it when it's already spent.

If you are new and small, a CPA may seem luxurious, but as you grow, investing in one will be the most important piece of the puzzle. Find a professional you can trust and call with questions, problems, and worries. You will not be sorry you did.

Operate Lean

Debt can be a useful tool in some business models—but for most small businesses, it's just a heavy chain. Operating lean means knowing what's essential and being brutally honest about what's not.

You don't need every software. You don't need that fancy office chair from Instagram. You need tools that *work*, and you need to be scrappy—especially in the early stages. I've watched businesses survive because they kept their overhead low, especially when revenue wasn't predictable. I've also watched promising brands crash because the debt load was just too high to breathe.

Try this: before you buy anything, ask yourself these questions:

- Will this make me money?
- Will this save me time I can spend making money?
- Do I already have something that can do this?

If it's not a *"Hell yes,"* it's probably a no.

Know Your Break-Even Number

This one might just save your sanity. Your break-even number is how much revenue you need to generate just to cover your expenses. Knowing this number isn't about fear—it's about freedom. When you know your minimum, you can make clear decisions. You stop spinning in panic. You start planning with power.

Let's say your monthly expenses are $3,200. That's rent, internet, supplies, software, etc. If you don't know that, every slow week will feel like failure. But if you *do* know that, you can reverse-engineer how many clients, sales, or services you need to meet it. Suddenly, your goals have structure—and structure breeds momentum.

Knowing your break-even number doesn't mean you're settling. It means you're steering. And steering, friend, beats drifting every single time.

Practical Tools

You don't have to love bookkeeping—but you do have to track your money. And thankfully, you don't need to be an accountant to do it well. Whether you're just starting out or already gaining momentum, using an accounting tool like **QuickBooks**, **Wave**, or **FreshBooks** will simplify your financial life tremendously. QuickBooks is the go-to for many—it's powerful, flexible, and accountant-friendly. Wave is a great free option, ideal for those in the early stages who need the basics without a monthly fee. FreshBooks offers something in between: a user-friendly design with helpful extras like time-tracking and invoicing, especially good for service-based businesses. The important thing isn't which one you choose—it's that you pick a system and *stick with it.* Don't rely on memory, sticky notes, or scattered receipts. Get your income and expenses into one place and let the software do the heavy lifting so you can focus on what you do best.

If you're still using your personal bank account to run your business, it's time to make a change. I say that with love and zero judgment—but also with urgency. Having a separate business checking account is non-negotiable. It protects you, keeps your books clean, and simplifies tax time like you wouldn't believe. Even if your revenue is small right now, creating this separation early sets a healthy foundation for everything that comes next. You'll know exactly what's coming in, what's going out, and how much runway you actually have—not what your personal balance *pretends* to show. Plus, if you ever want to apply for funding, bring on a partner, or grow your team, having clean business financials will put you light years ahead. No bells or whistles needed—just a separate account that says, "This is a real business."

Build in the habit that will help you stay ahead of the curve: a Monthly CEO Day. This isn't a day to serve clients or catch up on admin—it's a day to *lead.* Block out time once a month to check in with your business like it's a living, breathing thing. Review your income and expenses. Look at what worked and what didn't.

Update your content calendar. Adjust your goals. Shift your pricing if you need to. Light a candle, pour your favorite drink, and make it feel like a ritual—not a chore. It's a moment to zoom out from the daily grind and actually *see* your progress, your patterns, and your possibilities. Most financial fires aren't surprise explosions—they're slow burns we didn't notice. A CEO Day gives you the space to notice, to plan, and to steer your business with clarity and calm.

Finally, and most importantly: *Don't be afraid to charge what you're worth.* Let's talk about this. Not just what people are *willing* to pay, not just what feels "nice," but what your time, talent, and effort are truly *worth*. I know this is a hard one—especially when your work comes from a place of purpose. When you *care* about people, when you believe in generosity, when you're trying to build community or support others who are just starting out, it's easy to slip into the habit of saying yes to free gigs, discounted rates, or the infamous "exposure" opportunities. I've done it. More times than I care to count, and always because I wanted to be kind and generous.

In fact, for a long time, I was the example of what *not* to do. I meant well. I believed in showing up, in helping people, in saying yes. But behind the scenes? I was burnt out, carrying the weight of other people's expectations, and quietly resenting the imbalance. I had stretched myself too thin in the name of being generous—and ended up paying the price in stress, sleep, and sanity. That's when I learned something I now protect fiercely:

free is never really free. It always costs you something—time, energy, boundaries, mental bandwidth. And once someone has gotten something for free, it's hard to change the terms later.

These days, I'm much more careful about what I give away. I still believe in generosity, but now I practice it with wisdom. I ask: *Is this aligned with my mission? Am I in a season where I can afford to give this away without depletion? Will this lead to a healthy relationship, not just a one-sided transaction?* And most importantly, I remember that when I charge what I'm worth, I'm not just valuing my time—I'm modeling what it looks like to be a whole, sustainable, thriving professional. You can be kind and still have boundaries. You can love your work and still get paid. You can serve others without sacrificing yourself.

So if you needed permission: this is it. You are allowed to charge well. You are allowed to say no. And you are allowed to walk away from opportunities that look generous on the surface but drain you at the root.

Scaling

Scaling isn't about getting bigger. It's about getting *better.* Growing smart, growing steady, growing sustainably. Let's clear something up right now: *scaling doesn't mean blowing up your business overnight.* It's not about going viral, hiring ten employees, or building an empire by next Thursday. It's not even about doing *more*. It's about doing better—smarter, steadier, and more sustainably.

Scaling well means building a business that can breathe, grow, and thrive *without you needing to micromanage every single inch of it*. It's not a sprint. It's a long, steady walk toward something that can last.

So how do you know when you're ready to scale? You might be ready to scale if:

- You're maxed out on time and still turning away quality work.
- Your feel like your systems are held together with duct tape and desperation.
- You've proven your offer—but now the demand outpaces your capacity.
- You keep thinking, *"If I just had one more of me…"*
- You've built something people want… and now it's time to make it sustainable.

When you reach that point, here's the truth: growth without structure just creates chaos. And chaos is expensive—financially, mentally, and emotionally. So, before you scale, you need to build a foundation strong enough to hold the weight of what's coming.

Scaling Well Means:

Systems that save you hours. If you're doing the same task over and over again, create a system for it. Write it down. Record a quick screen share. Turn it into a checklist. Every repeated task should be repeatable *without you.* The goal isn't perfection—it's consistency. If it lives in your head, it can't grow. Get it out.

Delegation that doesn't scare you. This is a hard one, especially for those of us who built our businesses from scratch with sweat, tears, and way too many late nights. But at some point, you've got to let go. Scaling means trusting other people with parts of your process. That doesn't mean handing over the keys to your kingdom— but it does mean empowering others to handle what doesn't *need* to be done by you.

Saying no to good opportunities. This one's counterintuitive, but hear me out: when you're scaling, *focus* becomes your superpower. Not everything that glitters is gold for your business. Sometimes saying yes to one too many "good" opportunities will stretch you so thin that you have no bandwidth left for the *great* ones. Scaling is about discernment.

Streamlining your offers. More products or services doesn't mean more success. It usually means more confusion. Simplify. Focus on what works. Double down on your signature offer or best-seller. When people know exactly what you do—and why you're the best at it—it's easier for them to buy and easier for you to deliver.

Pricing for longevity—not just survival. If you're scaling, your pricing needs to reflect the *value* you offer and the *vision* you're building toward. Undervaluing yourself might get you quick wins, but it won't build a team, pay for tools, or allow you the rest you'll need in the long run. Sustainable pricing honors your time, your client, and your future.

Tools That Help You Scale:

One of the smartest moves you can make as a growing business owner is to stop relying on memory, sticky notes, and inbox chaos to keep everything afloat. Scaling isn't about doing more; it's about building systems that help you do what you already do—better, faster, and with far less stress. That's where a few key tools come into play, starting with something simple but game-changing: Standard Operating Procedures, or SOPs. These are your business's recipe cards—clear, step-by-step instructions for everything from sending invoices to onboarding clients. If you had to hand over a task tomorrow, an SOP would make sure someone else could do it without missing a beat. They're lifesavers when it comes to training new team members or just giving yourself a little mental breathing room.

Alongside SOPs, project management software like **Trello, Asana,** or **ClickUp** becomes your virtual brain. No more scattered to-do lists or forgotten deadlines. These tools let you organize projects, assign tasks, set due dates, and track progress in one central place. Whether you're working solo or with a team, they help you stay on top of the moving pieces without waking up at 3 a.m. wondering what you forgot.

To keep the client side of your business running smoothly, a solid CRM (Customer Relationship Management) platform like **HoneyBook** or **Dubsado** can become your command center. It houses your client information, contracts, invoices, communications— basically all the admin pieces that used to take you hours can now live in one streamlined, professional-looking system.

Automation is another piece of the puzzle that saves both time and sanity, especially during onboarding. Instead of manually sending welcome emails or trying to remember if you sent that intake form, you can build a simple automated sequence that greets every new client with the information they need, delivered right on time. It not only adds a level of polish to your process but also builds trust from day one.

Finally, don't underestimate the power of templates. Seriously. Any time you write an email, outline a proposal, post on social media, or explain your pricing— if you do it more than once, make a template. These reusable documents speed up your workflow and help you stay consistent in your messaging, no matter how busy things get.

All these tools and systems aren't about removing the human side of your business—they're about protecting it. When you're not buried in repetitive tasks, you can

focus on what you're best at: serving your clients well, thinking strategically, and creating with intention.
Scaling doesn't have to be a chaotic leap. With the right tools in place, it can be a smooth, intentional step toward more freedom, more impact, and a business that's finally working *with* you—not just because of you.

Here's the truth that no one puts in their six-figure webinar funnel: *scaling is less about strategy and more about surrender.*

You have to be willing to let go of control. To trust others. To shift from "I'll just do it myself" to "We can do this together." That's not weakness—it's wisdom. You're not meant to carry the whole thing forever. You're meant to *build something that can carry itself.*

So no, scaling isn't about size. It's about strength. And if you do it with heart, intention, and a willingness to loosen your grip just a little, you won't just grow— you'll grow *well.*

Some Things to Remember

- You are the biggest asset in your business—take care of yourself.
- Rest is not a luxury; it's a requirement.
- Slow growth is still growth.
- Don't chase numbers—chase impact.

- Your business will only be as healthy as your boundaries.
- God will open doors you didn't even know existed—just keep walking.

This is the practical part. The nuts and bolts. The "eat your vegetables" section of your entrepreneurial journey. But I want you to hear this with your whole heart: You can learn the skills. You can build the systems. You can become the leader you need to be.

And when you pair strategy with faith? There is nothing you cannot do with God's help.

Chapter 8

The Risk of Righteousness:

Lessons from Joseph of Arimathea

There comes a moment in every woman's journey—especially those of us building something bold, something lasting—when silence is no longer an option. A moment when the cost of staying in the good graces of the room we've outgrown outweighs the risk of stepping into the truth of who we really are.

Joseph of Arimathea understood that moment better than most.

He was a man of stature. A respected member of the Sanhedrin, the religious elite. A man who had proximity to power and the polished language of political survival. In modern terms, Joseph had the corner office, the seat at the table, the LinkedIn endorsements. He had built his reputation on alignment with the dominant narrative. But deep in his heart, something stirred—a loyalty to a truth that didn't fit the script.

He believed in Jesus. Quietly. Privately. Carefully.

That part of the story pierced me during a recent Easter service. Because it's a quiet form of torment many women know too well: managing the optics of belief while navigating a world that demands we dilute it. We walk the line, code-switch in meetings, shrink our voice so we don't seem "too much," all while secretly nurturing dreams and convictions that the world may not yet be ready to receive.

Joseph stayed silent while injustice bloomed. He played the long game of diplomacy while his soul whispered for something truer. And then came the crucifixion.

That was his line in the sand.

Not just the death of a man—but the death of Joseph's comfort. The moment when conviction could no longer be compartmentalized. When he realized that faith without courage is a beautifully decorated tomb.

So, he did the unthinkable.

He went to Pilate—to the very system that condemned Jesus—and asked for the body. It was more than logistics. It was rebellion wrapped in reverence. A man who once feared the consequences of association was now willing to stake his name, his network, and his legacy on a carpenter's dead son.

But the story didn't stop there.

Joseph didn't just bury Jesus. He buried a version of himself. The safe one. The curated one. The one who played by the rules of the room. He gave Jesus the tomb he had carved for himself—a final resting place. And in doing so, Joseph cracked open the beginning of resurrection.

That moment, that surrender, is a mirror for every woman daring to build her life with integrity.

Because there comes a time when we're asked to do the same. To give up the tombs we've carved for our egos—titles, roles, partnerships, approval—in order to honor what we are called to do. To choose calling over comfort. Conviction over convenience.

Maybe that's you right now.

Maybe you're a woman who's been working twice as hard to be seen half as much. Maybe you've bent yourself into impossible shapes to stay in the room, and now you're wondering what it might cost to speak plainly. To risk being misunderstood. To honor your values when it could cost you visibility.

Let me say this: what feels like loss is often the beginning of legacy.

Because what Joseph couldn't have known—what we often can't see when we're standing at the edge of risk—is that the tomb he surrendered would become the birthplace of the greatest miracle in history. The space he gave up became sacred ground.

The same is true for us.

When we give up the spaces that no longer serve who we are becoming, we make room for something divine to take root. When we let go of chasing favor and choose to walk in truth, we don't diminish our impact—we amplify it.

Joseph's story is more than a footnote in the resurrection narrative. It's a blueprint for everyone in business, in leadership, in life. Because we're not just building profit margins—we're building cultures. We're building freedom. We're building tables where others don't have to hide who they are to be invited to sit.

In a world that still rewards compliance and punishes authenticity, we need people who are willing to lead like Joseph. Women who will risk comfort for courage. Who will step forward when staying silent would be easier. Who will lay down legacy as it's been defined for them, in order to build legacy as it was meant to be—faithful, fierce, and free.

This isn't just inspiration. It's instruction. It's how we move forward every day: one brave choice at a time. One moment of truth-telling. One risk that says, "My purpose matters more than my polish."

So, if you find yourself at that threshold—don't stall.

Risk it.

Risk the room. Risk the reputation. Risk the well-worn path that no longer fits the person you are becoming. Because God never asks us to be perfect—He asks us to be faithful. And in the hollowed-out spaces we once called failure or fear, He brings resurrection.

That is how we rise.

Chapter 9

The Power of Community and Sisterhood

Before the sun lifted the dark from our little corner of the world, my friend Holly and I walked.

It'd become a ritual for a while—not just for movement or health, though those matter too—but something healthy in its stillness. Our steps fell in sync, breath rising in small clouds against the morning air, but the true rhythm is in our conversation. That's where the soul work lives. We talked about everything—our jobs, the jagged edges of society, the weight of family drama, and the exhaustion we often carry like second skin.

One morning, Holly spoke a truth that had clearly settled into her bones. She'd found herself in a situation where the folks she was focused on just were not hearing what she had to say. Their dismissive nature seemed intentional and was hurtful—and as strong as my friend was, it was chipping away at her worth. She—like so many of us—tried harder to get their approval, but it wasn't working. She paused and drew in a breath, in that raw and familiar way, "Why don't they like me?"

And just like that, I heard my twelve-year-old self speaking through her lips.

That question stings. It's innocent. It's universal. And it carries a kind of heartbreak only those who've asked it can understand. We walked silently for a moment under the weight of a sky still deciding whether to wake, and all I knew to say was, "Holly, those aren't your people."

It was the truth, wrapped in love—the kind of truth you learn only after years of trying to belong in spaces that were never meant for you. (Ask me how I know.)

As a woman in business—and just as a woman trying to move through this world with your spirit intact—there are few things more essential than finding your people. The right women. The ones who don't need explanations. Who show up early, stay late, and bring clarity or comfort depending on what the moment calls for. The ones who lace up their shoes to walk with you in the dark—not because they have to, but because they wouldn't be anywhere else.

Sometimes they're right beside you: a colleague, a neighbor, a friend in the stillness before dawn. Other times, you must find them through awkward bravery—a hesitant coffee invite, a message that says, "I admire you." It's rarely graceful. But it's always worth it.

The women in my life—like the ones in yours—have been my anchors, my lifelines, my launchpads. They've dropped off meals when life collapsed, picked up my kid when I was stuck, and reminded me of my worth when I couldn't see past my own disappointment. They've prayed with me through the darkest nights and danced when light finally broke through. They've called me out when I needed accountability, called me up when I needed encouragement, and called me beloved when I forgot I was anything close to worthy.

Holly's honest question reminded me that we all need that voice sometimes—the one that says, It's not you. It's them. And they aren't your people.

But more than that, we need the reminder that your people are out there.

They're the women who see you fully and still lean in. The ones who remind you that you're not too much and never not enough. The ones who don't just hear your pain but do their best to find good ways to soothe it.

And if you're blessed to have women like that in your circle, do not take it lightly. This is not a passive gift. It's an assignment. One that calls you to pay it forward, again and again, until every woman walking through the fog finds a hand to hold.

Business is hard. Life is harder. But when we build circles of women who carry each other through both— who walk before sunrise and after sunset—that's when we begin to change the world.

One foot in front of the other. One kind word. Sometimes, one morning walk at a time.

Because in business, especially, few things are more powerful than the presence of strong women who show up without being asked, who pour in without keeping score. When there's joy, they'll celebrate it like it's their own, and when it's gone, they will help you search for it.

These women will speak your name in rooms where opportunity lives. They'll send referrals, give honest feedback, and say, "You're not crazy" when nothing is going according to plan.

In my experience, they are nothing short of a gift. So where do you find them?

Sometimes they're obvious—right in front of you at church, in a business meeting, at the PTA table, or over a backyard barbecue. Other times, you have to be bold. You have to pick up the phone and introduce yourself and ask if you can buy them coffee. That's how some of my deepest friendships started—more stumble than swagger, but full of hope… and not once have I been turned away. Most women are just waiting for a real connection. We're all seeking a little more depth, a little more truth.

I've told you about my friend Diantha. But I need to tell you about some of the others, too.

There was a season in my life when I found myself in a combined fifth-and-sixth-grade classroom, holding a whiteboard marker in one hand and my unraveling life in the other. I hadn't dreamed of being a teacher. It wasn't a calling—it was a lifeline. A job I took because I needed health insurance and a paycheck, because bills don't wait for clarity or healing. I was exhausted—mothering and surviving. Each morning, I showed up for those 10- and 11-year-olds, praying they wouldn't see the cracks in me as I tried to keep their worlds steady while mine shook underneath.

That's when I met her: the vice principal with laugh lines around her eyes and Bible verses taped to the inside of her kitchen cabinets like scripture met sticky notes. Her home was humble and holy, filled with the scent of cornbread and conviction. She didn't need a pulpit—her life was the sermon. She never once told me what to do. She just offered coffee, quiet counsel, and a kind of unwavering faith that made me believe maybe I could keep going. When I questioned if I was ruining my kids or if I had the strength to rebuild, she'd hand me a plate, pat the seat beside her, and gently remind me that God's mercy shows up most in the mess.

Her advice wasn't flashy. It wasn't even advice most of the time. It was presence. It was truth spoken without judgment. It was her calm in the storm of my panic. She let me borrow her steadiness when mine was threadbare. I still remember the sound of her voice, steady as ever, saying, "You're not broken. You're just bending toward something new."

And then—like divine timing wrapped in postage stamps—there's the business colleague who always seemed to know when life got heavy. She wasn't loud about her kindness. She didn't make a show of it. But when my mother died and I didn't have enough money to get to the memorial, her card arrived like a miracle. Her handwriting. A folded $50 bill. "I hope this helps," she wrote. That's it. No grand gesture—just enough. Enough to get there. Enough to feel seen. She never stopped showing up. Another card came after surgery. Another for my second wedding; she bought the bouquet. She shows up with lunch, with laughter, with light. Sometimes, all it takes is seeing her name on the envelope to feel the fog lift. I love her more than she probably knows—and more than I'll ever be able to say aloud.

A youth minister once taught me how to drive—but it was never just about the car. It was about navigating life when you're unsure of the road, when your hands are trembling on the wheel. I was a teenager then, full of questions I was too afraid to ask out loud in most rooms. But not with her. With her, I could admit I didn't know what I believed, or if I believed at all. She never flinched. Never told me to hush or pray harder. She just listened, taught me how to parallel park, and quietly reminded me that God could handle my doubt. That kind of grace—the kind that lets you unravel without fixing you—stayed with me long after I got my license.

I have an aunt who's never raised her voice but somehow commands peace just by walking into a room. She's the version of myself I hope to become—older, wiser, still laughing at inappropriate jokes and making soup for people who didn't ask for it but desperately need it. When I call her in tears, she doesn't rush to rescue. She says, "Breathe. You're doing just fine." And she means it. Not in the way people say things to be nice, but in the way truth lands in your bones. When the ground has crumbled beneath me—and it has, more than once—she's reminded me that sometimes, the bravest thing you can do is not move. Just stand. Just breathe. Just stay.

Sue Ellen Riddle was a firecracker wrapped in pearls and unapologetic wisdom. She entered my life before everything fell apart—marriage, home, identity. At first,

I couldn't tell if she was brilliant or completely unhinged. Maybe she was both. The first time I asked someone at the clinic how she fit into the operation, they shrugged and said, "She doesn't really work here. She just helps people." And that was it. That was all I needed to know. It wasn't until much later I learned she'd co-founded the place but never claimed the title. She just got things done.

Sue Ellen didn't just pray—she moved. She made calls, filled gas tanks, bought diapers, raised money, opened doors. We ran errands together that turned into full-blown missions. Once, we drove all night to deliver a baby bassinet to a dingy motel at the top of a very steep mountain. That's the kind of woman she was. She lived like faith was a verb, not a feeling. She taught me that prayer was powerful—but action? That's where the holy lived. She changed me, deeply and forever. And to this day, when I'm unsure of what to do, I ask, "What would Sue Ellen do?" Then I smile, maybe cry a little, and try to do just a fraction of it.

But the deepest root in me—the one that still holds when the winds howl—belongs to my mother.

She didn't teach me to pray like it was an obligation. She prayed like it was oxygen. Like it was the only thing tethering her to this world while the cancer tried to take her out. She prayed over me when I ran wild. Prayed over the stove while dinner simmered. Prayed when she thought I couldn't hear, whispering my name in the same breath as Jesus. Even when she was too weak to walk, she prayed with her eyes closed and her fists clenched like she was fighting back the dark. And she was. She taught me that believing doesn't mean never doubting—it means showing up anyway. She was my anchor, my warrior, my example. Her faith soaked into me like rain on cracked earth.

These women—they're not just names in my story. They are the story.

They are why I can stand today, speak truth, run a business, raise a boy that might just change the world, rebuild after heartbreak, and hold space for others. They lifted me when I couldn't stand on my own. They reminded me that I was not alone. That I was never meant to be alone.

Because community isn't a luxury. It's not something we stumble into. It's something sacred, something designed by a God who knew we couldn't do life solo. We weren't built to carry the heavy alone.

So, if you're in a season where everything feels raw or broken—if you're rebuilding, if you're scared, if you're tired—don't isolate. Don't pretend you're okay when you're not. Find your people. They don't need to be many. Just a few who will stand in the fire with you and remind you where your strength comes from.

When women pour into each other like that—fierce and faithful, kind and unrelenting—miracles happen.

Business becomes purpose. Leadership becomes ministry. And life? Life becomes not just survivable but beautiful.

And I say this with love for the good men out there—truly—but every woman deserves a good circle of women. The kind who will show up with casseroles, bail money, childcare, and scripture in their back pockets. The kind who don't flinch when you say you're falling apart. Who say, "Okay. Let's fall together. And then we'll get up."

With them?

Everything is fuller. Lighter.

And far more beautiful.

Carry each other's burdens, and in this way, you will fulfill the law of Christ -Galatians 6:2

Chapter 10

Building Capacity

Finding your people? That's one thing. But building with them? Whew. That's where the real magic begins. Let's talk about hiring and teambuilding.

It's the shift from "Oh, she gets me" to "Let's build an empire together—preferably with matching mugs and at least one functioning printer." It's the move from recognition to relationship, from resonance to responsibility. And somewhere in that sacred, slightly chaotic in-between, something extraordinary starts to happen:

A group of individuals becomes a team.

And if you're really lucky? That team won't just be smart, skilled, or strategic. They'll be a little magical too. The kind of people who make you laugh at 10 a.m., cry at 10:30, or pull a miracle out of thin air by lunch. The kind who know when to bring coffee—and when to bring Kleenex.

You can't do everything forever, and you shouldn't try. Let's start with a little tough love: *you are not a machine.* You may be smart, scrappy, and fueled by caffeine and optimism—but you can't do *everything* forever. If you try, here's what happens: your energy tanks, your quality drops, and the dream you used to leap out of bed for? It starts to feel like a chain around your neck. Suddenly, the thing you built to give you freedom starts stealing your joy, your weekends, and your sleep.

Honestly, hiring too soon is its own kind of chaos. Bring someone on before your systems are ready, and you're not scaling—you're setting fires you now must pay someone else to put out.

So how do you know when it's time to hire? And how do you do it without turning your business into a bloated mess? Glad you asked.

Hire When:

You're consistently turning down work. If you keep finding yourself saying, "I'd love to, but I just don't have the bandwidth," it might be time to get help. A waitlist is great. A backlog so long that you dread opening your inbox? Not so great. That's a signal that your business is outgrowing your one-person, three-person, or 50-person operation.

You're doing $10/hour tasks when your time is worth $100/hour. Be honest: are you spending your mornings formatting invoices, updating Canva templates, or answering the same client question for the eighth time? Those are important tasks—but they're not the best use of your brain. If you're the visionary, stop acting like the unpaid intern. Hand off the $10 tasks so you can spend more time doing the high-value work that actually grows your business.

You're drowning, not swimming. A little hustle is normal. But if you feel like you're underwater all the time, missing deadlines, and forgetting what rest even feels like—you need help. It's not noble to run yourself into the ground. You don't get a medal for burnout. You get a therapist's invoice and a lot of regrets.

Start Small: Hiring doesn't have to mean full-time staff with benefits and birthday cakes. It can look like small, strategic steps that protect your energy *and* your bottom line. Here are some options you may not have thought of:

- *A virtual assistant* can take over admin tasks, inbox management, or scheduling. Suddenly, you have room to breathe—and to think.
- *A bookkeeper* will make you wonder why you ever tried to pretend you were a financial wizard. Your receipts will finally live somewhere other than your purse, and tax time won't feel like judgment day.
- *A part-time creative*—like a designer, copywriter, or social media manager—can take your content from "meh" to magnetic without you spending six hours debating which font feels most aligned with your soul.
- *A contractor for specialized tasks* means you're not trying to DIY your way through SEO or set up your website shopping cart at midnight while crying into your laptop. (We've all been there.)

Start with the one role that will buy you back the most time or relieve your biggest point of stress. It's not about making your life luxurious—it's about making it *livable*.

Here are a few additional pieces of advice on the subject. I promise they work wonders if you do it right.

Hire for character, train for skill. You can teach someone how to use your software or schedule your posts. What you *can't* teach is work ethic, kindness, and the ability to problem-solve without needing a pep talk every 20 minutes. Choose people who have the right attitude, the willingness to learn, and a heart that aligns with your values. That's your dream team material.

Don't micromanage—lead. If you're hiring someone only to watch over their shoulder and correct every comma, you're not delegating—you're babysitting. Set expectations clearly, offer support, and then *let go a little.* Leadership means equipping, not controlling. Trust is the soil that grows everything else.

Keep communication clear and consistent. Most work hiccups come from misaligned expectations, not malice. Use tools like Slack, Trello, or even a shared Google Doc to keep everyone in the loop. Have a weekly check-in. Clarify deadlines. Celebrate wins. Your team can only succeed if they know what success looks like.

Hiring is not about ego. It's about *sustainability*. It's about building something that lasts, something that grows, and something that doesn't require your fingerprints on every detail to keep moving forward. So, start small, start smart—but for the love of your sanity, *start*.

You were never meant to carry all this alone. Run the ad when the time is right.

What Makes a "Right" Team?

Spoiler alert: it's not about having the fanciest resumes or the most LinkedIn endorsements (though bless the overachievers—keep endorsing each other, ladies). The right team isn't built on perfect credentials. It's built on chemistry. On shared values. On a strange and beautiful balance of talents and temperaments.

The right team holds up mirrors for each other—not to point out the wrinkles, but to reflect back potential that might be hidden under burnout or bad lighting. They dust off old dreams and dare each other to dream new ones.

Take Abbey, for instance.

I've known Abbey since she was little—so bubbly she practically carbonated the room. Bright, curious, and genetically incapable of ignoring a stranger. She was made for sales, I thought. It was obvious. So, when she moved back to town after college, waiting tables while chasing a singing gig, I called her mama and said, "Let's make a move."

Abbey said yes. But she didn't end up in sales.

Turns out, God had other plans—and probably a good laugh, too. Abbey's now the architect of our online presence, crafting websites that somehow manage to be both technically brilliant and emotionally resonant. She makes code feel human. She's learning backend development, exploring SEO, and translating branding into visual poetry. It's not what she imagined, but it fits her like a second skin. We joke that God swerved on purpose. Abbey's joy isn't loud—it's rooted, and it's blooming.

And then there's Hannah.

Abbey's work bestie. Our quiet storm. She came to us as an intern—young, polite, and slightly terrified of calling anyone on the telephone. Fast forward, and she's a mama-in-the-making, with a camera in one hand and a vision in the other. Hannah sees light in places others overlook. She captures moments that make you pause. She's learning to trust not just her lens, but her voice. Watching that unfold? Priceless.

Now, Ellen—our spreadsheet whisperer.

While the rest of us are off dreaming big dreams or making creative messes, Ellen is color-coding our chaos into something resembling strategy. She doesn't just organize—she orchestrates. Deadlines, deliverables, digital systems? All humming in tune because Ellen willed them into harmony. She's our logistical lighthouse in the fog of a Monday morning.

They each bring something irreplaceable.

Abbey's imagination.
Hannah's artistry.
Ellen's structure.

They don't just work together. They believe in one another.

They fill each other's gaps, finish each other's sentences, and send each other TikToks that make me question our productivity levels—but somehow, the work gets done. And not just done. Done beautifully. Done with heart.

Our team will continue to grow, and these are the women who started the movement.

This isn't just business. This is fellowship.

It's showing up on the hard days with grace and caffeine. It's finishing the project and noticing someone hasn't eaten all day. It's texting a reminder that says, "You've got this," before the big pitch. It's balancing illness and invoices, laughter and leadership, and soon enough it will also be balancing babies and deadlines, new relationships and old obligations, and tempering the highs and lows of training new team members with respect in what we all believe is one of the best jobs on earth.

Business owners—especially ones trying to build something out of thin air—deserve a circle that doesn't just cheer for their success but also contributes to it. People who remind them that dreaming big isn't frivolous. It's faithful.

When a community links arms and builds together, what happens isn't just productive. It's legacy-making.

So, here's to your team—the one you're building, the one you've found, or the one you're still praying for.

May they be brilliant, brave, slightly chaotic, and wildly kind. May they build beside you, dream with you, and hold you up when the weight if it all gets heavy.

Because with them?

Life can be richer. Business can be holier. And the journey? It can be far more beautiful.

A strong team isn't just about filling roles. It's about seeing people—sometimes before they fully see themselves. It's about recognizing that someone might have come in the door as a "maybe," but with the right encouragement, the right space, and a little time, they become something indispensable.

That's the art of building. It's less like hiring and more like curating a garden. You plant seeds, not all of which you recognize at first. Some bloom early. Some take longer. But the right team? They tend to each other's growth. They don't compete—they conspire for good.

In this garden, trust is the soil. Not just "I trust you to do your job," but "I trust you to care as much as I do." Trust is built in the small things: the check-in after a tough week, the shared silence over coffee, the moments when someone steps up before you ask.

It's what allows you to take risks, to have hard conversations, to push each other toward something better without fear that someone's going to pull away when things get real.

And it's what lets a former maybe-salesperson become a digital architect. What lets an intern become an artist. What lets an operations maven keep it all from falling apart.

You'll know when you've built the right team. It won't be because the calendar is flawless or every project is perfect. You'll know it in the laughter echoing down the hallway. In the grace they give each other. In the weird inside jokes that no one else understands but somehow hold everything together. The right team isn't just about output. It's about synergy, creativity, and shared belief in something bigger than the sum of its parts.

Most of all, you'll know because, even when things are hard, you won't want to do it with anyone else.

Great things in business are never done by one person. They're done by a team of people.

—Steve Jobs

As iron sharpens iron, so one person sharpens another.
— Proverbs 27:17 (NIV)

Chapter 11

Running a Business That Honors Our Values

Your clients are the lifeblood of your business—but they're also human. Some will adore you. Some will test your patience. And all of them, in one way or another, will teach you something about how you show up, where your boundaries are, and what kind of leader you truly want to be.

In the early days of your business, you'll probably say yes to everyone. Every inquiry, every project, every awkward consultation that makes your stomach tighten—you'll take it all. Because that's what we're told to do, right? Hustle. Serve. Prove yourself. We smile through discomfort and call it "paying dues." But here's what I wish someone had told me sooner: *you can love people well without letting them run you ragged.* Boundaries aren't unkind. They're protective. They're what make sustainable service—and sanity—possible.

Let's start with the golden rules, the non-negotiables for client relationships that protect both parties and create space for mutual respect. First, *have a contract—every single time.* Not because you expect things to go wrong, but because clarity protects everyone. It sets the tone. It communicates, "I take this seriously." Second, *communicate expectations clearly and early.* Spell out deliverables, timelines, boundaries, and your process. Third, remember: *underpromise and overdeliver—but not at the expense of your health.* Showing up strong doesn't mean burning yourself out. And finally, this: *if a client drains your soul, release them with kindness.* Grace and boundaries are not mutually exclusive.

… One of the most powerful lessons I learned the hard way is that *not every client is your person—and that's okay.* There will be clients who micromanage, criticize, ignore your expertise, or demand more than what's fair. You'll feel the tension before you can name it. That gut-check before a phone call. That energy drop every time their name shows up in your inbox. You'll start to dread the work and eventually question your own worth. That's your cue. You don't have to wait until something dramatic happens. If you know it's not working, let them go. Kindly, professionally, and without apology. Offer a referral if you can. Don't gossip. But *do not stay out of guilt.* Because your peace, your energy, your mission—they matter more than any paycheck.

Here's a short but mighty list of when it's time to release a client:

- If they're verbally or emotionally abusive.
- If they don't benefit from what you offer.
- If they don't understand—or respect—what you do.
- If they monopolize your time and drain your energy.
- If your gut says, "This isn't right."
- If they pick fights or make you question your competence.

Let them go. Seriously. Let them go.

And while you're doing that, *nurture the clients who do align with you.* The good ones—the kind, grateful, respectful ones—deserve your care and attention. Send a welcome packet that makes them feel seen. Follow up monthly with updates and check-ins, even if they're brief. Express gratitude often. Remember their birthdays. Be human. Because business isn't robotic—it's relational. Relationships, especially in small business, are the difference between surviving and thriving.

Your best clients won't expect perfection—they'll appreciate integrity. They'll cheer for you, refer you, and treat you like a partner, not a servant. Those are your people. Hold onto them. Build with them. And when you have to draw a boundary, or even say goodbye to someone, remember *you are not just running a business—you are creating a life.* One filled with respect, intention, and space to breathe.

So, love people. Serve them well. But never forget that *you* matter, too.

Client Care Tips:

So, how do you love your clients *well*, without losing your mind? Here are a few small but powerful practices:

Send a Welcome Packet. It doesn't have to be fancy. A PDF with a friendly intro, what to expect, communication preferences, and your working hours is enough. It sets the tone. It says, "I'm organized. I care. And I'm here to support you."

Send Monthly Updates. Even if nothing big has changed, checking in builds trust. A quick "Hey, just wanted to touch base and let you know where we are in the timeline!" goes a long way toward avoiding awkward "Where is this?" emails.

Say Thank You—Often. Send a handwritten note. Drop a voice message. Shout them out on social media (with permission). Clients who feel appreciated are more likely to refer you, respect your time, and come back for more.

Be Human. If your kid gets sick or your power goes out, or your brain needs a break—say so. You're not a robot. You're a person doing your best. Transparency, paired with professionalism, creates connection.

The first time I wrote a multi-thousand-dollar refund check to a client, I cried.

Not the kind of delicate, Instagram-worthy crying either. I mean the full-body, breathless, "I might throw up" kind. And actually? I did. I threw up. Not from guilt— but from the pressure of holding together a business, a team, a reputation, and a standard of excellence… while being disrespected in broad daylight.

It wasn't just the money. It was what that money represented: all the long nights, the creative labor, the earnest effort to meet a client where he was—even when he made it nearly impossible.

He was a young restaurant owner, charismatic on the surface. He hired us for multiple projects with big talk and bigger promises. From day one, it was chaos. He'd text us at 2 a.m. with half-baked thoughts and scattered voice memos. No clear goals. No branding direction. And God help us if we asked real business questions. He'd sidestep every single one like it was a game of dodgeball.

And the kicker? If we needed to photograph food for marketing—his food, for his business—he refused to provide anything. We were expected to pay for the meals ourselves, up front. Sometimes the dishes cost more than the project deposit.

But still, we showed up.

My team—brilliant, kind, overqualified humans— pushed through. They built a website from scratch. Ran ad campaigns. Wrote content. Polished brand copy. They worked late, skipped lunches, poured their talent into a business that didn't seem to want to succeed, but expected to be carried across the finish line anyway.

Until one day, I'd had enough.

We had a looming deadline. A major campaign waiting on final approval. No response to several important and significant questions. So, I did what I'd never done before: I got in my car and drove straight to the restaurant, hoping for five minutes of clarity. I walked in, made eye contact with him across the dining room— and watched him physically duck into the kitchen.

I asked an employee if I could speak with him. She disappeared into the back and returned with a straight face and a lie: "He's not here today. Won't be back this week."

And I stood there, stunned, but not surprised.

Later that night, I received an email from him. It wasn't just unkind—it was vile. Full of profanity. Demeaning. Dismissive. Disrespectful to my staff in a way that made my blood boil. He belittled the very people who had moved mountains trying to help him grow his business while he played ghost.

That was the moment.

I opened our accounting software, added up every cent he'd ever paid us, and wrote a refund check on the spot. A few thousand dollars, just like that—gone. My stomach turned. Payroll was coming. Bills were looming. But I handed that check over like it was oxygen.

Because here's what I knew in my bones: No amount of money is worth disrespect. No contract is worth compromising your integrity. And no client—no matter how "promising"—is worth sacrificing the dignity of your people.

I didn't just write a check that day. I reclaimed my peace. I chose my people. I backed my values with action. And I'd do it again in a heartbeat. In that instant, a new company policy was born: *At Kellum Creek, we don't do crazy.*

Now, I know that might sound blunt, maybe even unprofessional if you like your boundaries dressed in corporate jargon. But it's not just an internal tagline. It's a line in the sand.

If a client brings chaos into our space—if they weaponize urgency, sow discord, manipulate communication, or stir up drama—we show them to the door. With kindness, but without apology.

This business was built to be a safe place, a place that magnifies the good work of our clients, of our own, and of the people and organizations in this community we support.

As for the people who show up here every day, the people who pour their talent, their time, and their hearts into making this business work: I owe them more than a paycheck. I owe them protection.

Our values are not aspirational posters on a wall. They're lived, enforced, and yes, sometimes expensive.

But I'd rather be broke with integrity than rich and out of alignment.

And honestly? We weren't broke for long.

That refund wasn't the end—it was a clearing. And in that cleared-out space, better clients came. Respectful ones. Aligned ones. Clients who trust the process and honor the partnership. The kind who see what we do and say, "Yes, let's build something beautiful together."

So, to every woman out there running a business, leading a team, carrying the invisible load of everyone else's expectations—I see you. And I want to tell you something no one tells us enough: You're allowed to walk away from money that costs you your peace. You're allowed to write the check, close the door, and move on. You are not too much for asking to be treated with respect. And the minute you start enforcing that boundary? That's the minute you start building not just a business, but a legacy.

Kellum Creek wasn't built overnight. And it sure as heaven wasn't built by accident.

In case you are still looking for the magic spell: This isn't one of those "I fell into success" stories. There was no miraculous business loan, no viral launch, no secret formula whispered over lattes. We continue to build the old-fashioned way—one client, one late night, one hard-earned lesson at a time. This team will build while kids are sleeping, build while bills are due, build with laptops on kitchen tables and prayers whispered between phone calls.

But more than that? We will continue to build on purpose. With purpose. For a purpose.

Because I have never just wanted a business that made money. I want a business that makes sense. A business that doesn't just show up on paper but shows up in people's lives. One that aligns with who I am, what I believe, and—most importantly—Who I ultimately answer to.

For me, that means building something that honors God. Not just in the headline moments or the shiny success stories. But in the quiet, often-unseen choices that don't make it to social media.

It shows up in the decisions nobody claps for:

- Choosing honesty when a shortcut would be faster.

- Paying vendors before paying myself.

- Sending the email that says, "We fell short—and here's how we'll make it right."

- Having the hard conversation instead of ghosting.

- Saying no to big money when the values don't line up.

This is where the nitty-gritty lives. It's not glamorous, but I hope it's the faithful stewardship of what I've been trusted to build. Because if I can't honor God in the little things, what am I even doing with the big ones?

At Kellum Creek, success doesn't look like corner offices or industry awards–of which there have already been a few (though if more come, great—we'll take them gratefully and probably make a Canva graphic). Success, for us, looks like integrity on the days no one's watching. It looks like serving clients with excellence and treating our team with reverence. It looks like protecting peace, pursuing justice, and building beauty into the bones of our work.

We've cried over invoices. Prayed over pitches. Laughed until we couldn't breathe because sometimes that's the only thing keeping us from crying again. But through it all, we've stayed rooted in purpose. I pray we continue along that path.

This is not a side hustle. It's not a steppingstone. It's not a vanity project. Kellum Creek is a calling. And we treat it like one.

We show up every day not just to earn, but to honor.

So, if you're building something of your own—something that feels small, slow, completely incomplete—I want you to know you have not lost your mind. You're just building with intention. And yes, it's harder that way. But it's also the right way.

Because when you build with purpose, you don't just create products or services. You create impact. You build trust. You build legacy. You build something that can weather the storm because its foundation is not made of ego or trends—it's made of truth.

So no, Kellum Creek isn't happening overnight. And no, it's not happening by accident.

It happening because God whispered something into my heart, and I decided to listen—one brave, trembling yes at a time.

Let me be clear:
Faith isn't something I sprinkle on top of this business like powdered sugar on a donut. It's not a decorative flourish or a clever tagline. It's the foundation.

It's the reason I started this company, and it's the reason I stay when the pressure mounts and the world says, "Just compromise a little." It's the reason we treat people the way we do. The reason we draw certain lines. The reason we turn down lucrative contracts that don't sit right in our spirit—even when the numbers look good and the timing looks perfect.

I will say it again: if the peace isn't there, we walk away. If the alignment's off, we let it go. If it costs us integrity? It costs too much.

Faith is why we don't badmouth our competitors, even when the opportunity is tempting and the receipts are damning. It's why we don't just take on projects because they pay—we take them on because they fit, because they feel purposeful, because they're a match not just in branding but in values.

Faith is why we fiercely protect our team—not just from burnout, but from toxic clients, frantic energy, and anything that threatens the culture of support we've worked so hard to build.

It's why we believe—deeply—that you can lead with kindness and still be respected. That you can extend grace without being seen as weak. That you can run a generous, people-centered business and still be profitable, still be professional, still be powerful.

We believe that excellence and empathy aren't mutually exclusive. That strategy and spirit can co-exist. That success isn't just about scale—it's about substance.

And listen, I know there are spaces where bringing up God or goodness makes people nervous. Where faith is seen as a liability or a liability in disguise. But for me? Faith isn't something I keep separate, compartmentalized in a corner of my life, pulled out on Sundays or when I need a miracle.

It flows through everything. Every client we serve. Every decision we make. Every invoice, every email, every late-night brainstorming session.

We're not just building something good. We're building something true. Something rooted.

And if that makes us stand out? Good. I'd rather stand out for the right reasons than blend in for the wrong ones.

So, if you're out there trying to build a business with both a backbone and a soul—keep going. You don't need to water down your faith to make your business palatable. You don't need to choose between belief and brilliance. You can build something bold because of your faith, not in spite of it.

And when you do? You won't just build income. You'll build impact. And that changes everything.

There are moments—more than I care to count—when I don't know what to do. When the numbers don't add up. When the inbox is full but I feel more exhausted and emptier than not. When the path ahead is unclear, and I can't tell if I'm walking in faith or just fumbling in the dark.

Those are the moments I pray. Not just for answers, but for alignment. Because the older I get, the more I realize I'm not looking for shortcuts—I'm looking for center. For confirmation that the next step, however small, is the right one. That I'm not just building something that works on paper, but something that honors the posture of my heart.

Most days, I write my prayers down. Sometimes in a quiet corner. Sometimes scribbled on the back of a receipt or a Post-it note in the car. *Write it out. See it laid bare.* A lesson from one of the wisest men I've ever encountered. That's become my rhythm. My reminder. My way through.

I pray for wisdom. For peace that doesn't depend on the bank account. For courage to say no when everything in me wants to say yes—just to keep the peace, or the client, or the illusion of stability. For strength to choose people over profit. And for humility—to own it when I get it wrong. To fix it. To grow.

Because I don't want to build a business that looks successful from the outside but feels hollow on the inside. I want to build something that feels whole. That reflects the fruit of the Spirit—not just in theory, but in practice:

Love. Joy. Peace. Patience. Kindness. Goodness. Faithfulness. Gentleness. Self-control.

Even when it's hard. *Especially when it's hard.*

And if it sounds like I'm asking God for a lot—you're right, I am. But I've also seen Him show up. Not once. Not occasionally. *Repeatedly.* He has parted the waters when I was out of options. He has provided the check, the clarity, the comfort—sometimes all three in the same afternoon. He has whispered yes when I doubted, and no when I begged, and given grace when I didn't even know I needed it.

This isn't just business to me. Make no mistake: faith lives here.

When a new opportunity comes in, I ask for discernment. When a client relationship turns rocky, I ask for direction. When I'm tempted to take the easy way out, I ask for a better way. His way. Because at the end of the day, I don't just want to be known for what we build—I want to be known for how we built it.

I believe we're doing business the way God intended—where excellence and ethics go hand in hand. Where grace isn't weakness—it's the framework. Where clients feel seen, not sold to. Where work feels less like a hustle and more like honoring the call.

Yes, you can make a living. Yes, you can build a brand. Yes, you can scale and grow and lead, but you don't have to lose your soul doing it. You can lead with kindness and still be respected. You can build with conviction and still be wildly creative. You can run a company that doesn't just thrive financially, but flourishes spiritually. So, if you've ever wondered whether it's possible to run a business that feels like grace in motion—let me tell you, it is. I know, because I'm living it.

And not a day goes by that I don't thank God for the privilege to do so.

Chapter 12

Legacy

I want to tell you a little bit about what legacy means to me, and that story is wrapped up completely in a woman who God gave me years ago. I've already mentioned her once in this book, and the truth is–though she has passed away–she is still a very big part of my life. Her name was Sue Ellen Riddle.

Some people leave behind fortunes; others leave behind legacies. Sue Ellen Riddle never made headlines, never had children of her own, and didn't leave me anything you could deposit in a bank—but what she gave me was far more valuable.

Sue Ellen was the kind of woman who didn't just talk about kindness—she practiced it with her hands and her heart. She fed the hungry without making it a spectacle. Quietly slipped shoes on bare feet. Stood between danger and the vulnerable with a kind of defiance I cannot begin to describe and would hate to be on the wrong side of. And she loved unlovable and desperate people—the sort of love that asks nothing in return, the kind that shows up when you think nothing will.

The Good Lord knows she showed up for me repeatedly.

When I left my marriage with only the clothes I was wearing, shaken and unsure, Sue Ellen met me at a kitchen table with a hot plate of food. She didn't ask questions. She just walked through the back door at a peaceful place where she knew I could start to heal and started making space for peace. She didn't try to fix anything. She just sat in the wreckage with me until I could breathe again.

When I lost my job and with it, my sense of purpose, Sue Ellen made her opinion of the decision known to those who'd made it and then called or came to see me every day to make sure I was surviving. Sometimes, she brought dinner. Sometimes, she brought clothes. Sometimes, she just brought riotous old stories to remind me how to laugh.

When I opened my business, when I dared to believe in something new, Sue Ellen showed up again, and often. She brought artwork for my office walls, snacks, and a rug. She'd rescue me from whatever administrative task I was eyeball-deep in for the day and ferry me to lunch. "You're doing it," she said. "You don't need those crazy people anyway."

Her love and support are the riches I carry. I hope whole-heartedly that the way I run my business is rooted in Sue Ellen's spirit, that I show up, that I take care of people, that I remember that success isn't about what I gain, but what I give. Every decision, every client, every risk—I carry her legacy into all of it. Not because I have to. Because I want to be the kind of person she believed I could be.

Sometimes when we lose the people we love the most, they leave us tangible things, but she left me more: a blueprint for a life well-lived. And that's worth everything.

At the end of the day, I'm not trying to be remembered for having the fastest turnaround times or the most efficient systems (though we do love a good workflow). I'm not building a legacy of checklists or KPIs or even glowing testimonials. I want something deeper. Something truer– that sounds a little crazy for a marketing firm, but I really do want people to say, "She honored God in the way she did business."

That's it. That's the measure. That's the win.

I want my team to feel valued—not just for what they produce, but for who they are when they show up, exhausted or elated, brilliant or struggling. I want my clients to feel seen, not just as billable hours or brand names, but as real people with real dreams and real lives behind the inbox.

And I want my community—this beautiful, messy, growing network of people we serve and partner with— to feel the ripple effect of a company that's trying, however imperfectly, to reflect something good in a world that is a whole lot less than perfect.

Because if we get everything else "right" but miss that? We've missed the point and it's the only kind of success I'm chasing.

And if you're reading this, trying to build something meaningful—whether you're just starting out or knee-deep in the trenches—I want you to know this:

Your business can reflect your faith, your values, your voice, and the people who made you who you are. It can be a force for good, not just for profit. It can be generous and wildly successful. It can be humble and deeply impactful. You don't have to separate who you are from what you build. You just have to choose to build differently.

That choice won't always be easy—but it will always be worth it.

Now, let me step up on one of my favorite soapboxes.

Want to know one of the fastest ways to get on my nerves? Ask any of my team. They'll tell you: I'm incredibly patient—until you start badmouthing others in our industry.

We know who our competitors are. We know who's doing beautiful work in our space. We've seen the brands they've built, the campaigns they've launched, the communities they've nurtured. And truth be told? Some of them are really good at what they do.

And that doesn't threaten me one bit.

If I overhear someone on my team bragging on a competitor? I love that. I'll stop mid-coffee-sip to listen. Because that tells me we're secure in who we are. That we don't need to diminish others to validate our own value. That we can celebrate excellence—even when it doesn't come with our name on it.

But tearing people down to prop ourselves up? *Absolutely not.* That's not our way. That's not the kind of leadership I believe in. And that's certainly not the kind of business I'm trying to build. We don't sling mud to climb mountains.

We believe in the power of rising with integrity, not at the expense of others.

"When they go low, we go high." That phrase is written on the white board behind my desk. It is attributed to Michelle Obama, and whatever your politics are, you should write it down somewhere. It's not just a quote we hang on the wall—it's something we live, every single day. In our team meetings. In our client conversations. In the way we talk when no one else is listening.

The way you speak about others is a mirror of how you see yourself. When you're secure in your mission, aligned in your purpose, and rooted in faith—you don't have to tear anyone down. You can build your house with open hands and a wide heart. And when you do? You build something really worth remembering.

Let's get something straight:
At Kellum Creek, we don't force the fit.

I've already spoken to this, but it bears repeating. We don't twist ourselves into knots trying to make mismatched client relationships work. We don't pretend a project feels right when it's already rubbing wrong. We don't ignore red flags just because the check cleared.

Sometimes it's values that don't align. Sometimes it's communication style—scattershot requests, 2 a.m. texts, or worse, radio silence when the deadline looms. Sometimes it's a sense—deep in the gut—that no matter how much strategy or creative brilliance we pour in, it won't be enough to shift the foundation of disconnection. When that happens, I pause. Quickly. Clearly. Kindly.

Sometimes that means refunding the money. Sometimes it means referring the client to a competitor we trust—someone whose process or personality may be a better fit. And always, always, it means choosing what's right over what's easy.

Because here's what I believe with my whole heart: We don't take money we haven't earned. We don't waste anyone's time—not ours, not theirs. And we don't keep clients we can't serve with excellence.

If we can't elevate your brand, sharpen your message, or help you shine in a way that feels true to who you are—we will bow out, with grace and gratitude, and cheer you on as you find the team that can.

This isn't about ego. It's about ethic. It's about doing business with integrity, not desperation.

And it's about trusting that the clients who are meant for us—the aligned ones—will see our heart, not just our portfolio, and say, "Yes. These are my people."

Chapter 13

Culture

Now let's talk about culture—because it's not just about who we hire. It's also about who we serve.

The culture of our workplace is a living, breathing thing. It's delicate, an organism that needs to be fed and loved. And it doesn't just depend on the energy inside our walls—it's shaped by the energy we allow through the door.

Which means we're careful. We're careful about the clients we say yes to. We're thoughtful about the energy they carry. Because energy is contagious. Drama is like mold—it spreads quietly, grows quickly, and before you know it, it's eating away at creativity, collaboration, and peace. So, we don't do drama. We just don't.

That doesn't mean we expect people to be perfect. Far from it. We expect humanity, not perfection. We expect respect, clear communication, and a basic commitment to mutual care. We believe in honest conversations, in space for learning, in room to grow. But we also believe in boundaries.

We will open the door wide for collaboration, grace, and meaningful work. And we'll close that same door—kindly but firmly—if the peace of our team, the heart of our culture, or the health of our process is at risk.

Because our team? They matter too much. The work? We love it enough to protect it. And our calling? It's too important to be compromised by chaos.

So, if you're a fellow business owner trying to figure out where the line is—this is it:

You're allowed to protect your peace.
You're allowed to choose alignment over accommodation.
You're allowed to say, "We're not the right fit," and still believe in someone's success elsewhere.

It's not weakness. It's discernment.
And it will save your business—and your sanity—in more ways than one.

You can write the mission statement. You can design the brand. You can hang the vision on the wall in shimmering gold foil. But if your team doesn't believe it, live it, and protect it? None of it lasts.

At Kellum Creek, our values aren't mine alone. They belong to us. They're lived out in every client call, every brainstorm session, every late-night deadline sprint with snacks and sarcasm. They show up in Trello messages that say, "You good?" and in quiet moments of grace no one sees.

Our people didn't just say yes to a job—they said yes to a culture. A culture of kindness, of integrity, of consistency. A culture that does work that doesn't just look good—but feels good in your soul.

This team understands that we don't just serve brands—
we serve humans. That's the mission.

They show up with grit and grace, day after day. They
build beauty from blank slates. They hold boundaries
with compassion, and say, "We're not the right fit," with
more love than most people offer in their contracts.

They protect the peace of this place like it's sacred—
because it is. They uplift one another like it's second
nature. They lead by example—especially when no one's
watching.

And if you ask me what it really means to honor your
values? It's that.

It's not just saying the right things when the camera's
on. It's doing the right things when the room is quiet and
no one's giving you credit.

That's what makes our business strong. That's what
makes our culture unshakable. That's what turns a small
team into something mighty.

Chapter 14

Faith is Your Compass

Let me tell you a story.

It's fresh—still tender in the way only unanswered prayers and hard goodbyes can be. But I think it's worth sharing, because chances are, you've been here too. Holding a door that's already closed. Praying for clarity while quietly hoping God agrees with your plan.

A few weeks ago, I sat alone in my office, staring at a client account that had gone silent. Not just quiet—dead air. No communication. No payments. No explanation. Just months of silence stacked on top of unpaid invoices and mounting tension I could feel in my chest every time I opened my inbox.

I finally got a meeting on the books. And before it started, I did what I always do when I'm out of answers and running on grace fumes: I prayed.

"God, if we're supposed to continue this project, fling the doors wide open. And if we're not—please, make it unmistakably clear."

That was it. I wasn't praying for miracles or money—I just wanted clarity. The kind that doesn't whisper, but echoes. The kind you can't talk yourself out of later.

The meeting came. I showed up fully, honestly. I laid it all out on the table—what we'd delivered, what we needed from them, why we had hit pause. I spoke with compassion, but also with backbone. Because I run a small business. I pay real people with real families. I can't fund work that no one else is funding and call that "hope." That's not faith—that's poor stewardship.

To my surprise, they were receptive. Apologetic, even. A few days later, a partial payment came in—not everything, but enough to spark hope. Enough to suggest maybe this thing still had life in it.

So, I leaned back in. I rolled up my sleeves and got to work. We'd been handling their SEO (search engine optimization, or for those who aren't in the know, getting websites to rank higher on Google or other search engines)—it's not sexy. It's not fast. It's the unglamorous, behind-the-scenes kind of work that makes or breaks visibility for business. It's also slow, cumulative, and invisible… until it isn't.

That weekend, I camped out in my office. I made backend improvements, cleaned up schema, rewrote metadata—work no one ever sees but that shifts the algorithmic tide over time. Late Sunday night, exhausted but satisfied, I hit "send" on an update.

A few hours later, their reply landed like a slap: "But why haven't you done anything until now?"

I sat there blinking at the screen, gut-punched. Confused. Hurt. A little stunned.

I responded with as much grace and clarity as I could muster. I reminded them of the unpaid invoices. The paused work. The face-to-face meeting in their own boardroom where we all nodded in agreement.

The next morning, I got a call. One of the decision-makers said flatly, "You haven't done a thing for us. We're moving on."

And just like that, it was over.

I wasn't devastated. Not in the way you are when you lose something precious. But I was stunned. Because they knew better. We had the conversations. The proof. The paper trail. The integrity.

And then I realized: I had prayed for clarity. And God delivered. He didn't whisper. He didn't nudge. He shut that door so hard it echoed through my week. And in that quiet moment, I felt it—like a holy exhale: "This is the answer you asked for."

I could have fought it. Drafted the long email. Attached receipts, screenshots, timelines. Demanded fairness. But instead, I whispered, "Thank You."
…and I walked away.

Because sometimes, faith in business doesn't look like a win. Sometimes, it looks like obedience that costs you something. Sometimes, it's closing your laptop and choosing peace over pride. Sometimes, it's trusting that God's "no" is protection, not punishment.

I have been entrenched in King Solomon lately. Here is the verse that keeps coming back to me– our pastor has even done a couple of sermons on it recently.

"The prudent see danger and take refuge, but the simple keep going and pay the penalty."
— Proverbs 22:3 (NIV)

So, no, I didn't expect the door to close. Not that one.

It's a strange feeling—watching something shut down that you never should've opened in the first place but somehow found yourself fighting to keep alive. I was confused. And if I'm honest, a little in awe. Not of the situation itself, but of how clearly God was saying, *"No more."*

That's the kind of clarity only He can provide.

The project seemed promising. The client looked like a good fit. On paper, everything was lining up. But in my spirit? There was friction. And when God finally pulled the plug, there was relief—and a quiet rebuke: *Why were you still holding the door open after I'd told you to let go?*

Some versions of Proverbs 22:3 say the wise "hide themselves," or "take cover." In other words—they *stop.* They don't double down. They don't slap a motivational quote on the wall and bulldoze ahead. They listen. They recognize the signs. They protect their peace. They obey.

But the simple-minded?

They ignore it. They call it "grit." They press forward and fall face-first into consequences that wisdom tried to help them avoid.

I've done that. More times than I want to admit.

We don't always miss danger because we're blind. Sometimes we see it and keep walking anyway because pride is louder than wisdom. Or we've grown so confident in our expertise that we forget who gave us the ability in the first place.

Let's be clear: *expertise is not enough.*

You can be the best in your field. You can have every certification, every accolade, every bit of data at your fingertips, and still make a foolish choice because your foundation isn't built on God—it's built on *you.*

That's the danger.

Proverbs 3:5 says:

> *"Trust in the Lord with all your heart and*
> *lean not on your own understanding."*

It's a gentle verse with a fierce command: *Don't lean on yourself.*

Because you don't know what's coming. Your resume doesn't see tomorrow. Your knowledge doesn't catch every nuance. Your gut can be wrong. And when we trust ourselves more than we trust God, we are walking headfirst into unnecessary pain.

Even Solomon—the man who literally *asked God for wisdom*—got this wrong.

You know the story. God came to Solomon in a dream and said, *"Ask me for anything."* He could've asked for wealth, power, revenge, status—but he asked for wisdom. And God was so pleased, He not only gave Solomon what he asked for, but more than he imagined.

But wisdom doesn't immunize you from disobedience. It's not a free pass to do life without God.

Solomon made alliances by marrying lots of foreign women—daughters of kings whose gods were not his God. On the surface, it was brilliant politics. Strategic partnerships. Global expansion. But it wasn't what God told him to do.

And over time, those "wise" decisions pulled his heart away. The kingdom fractured. His legacy was tainted. And it all began the moment he stopped asking what God thought and started leaning on his own understanding.

If Solomon needed God for every decision, so do we.

Don't let your intelligence become your idol. Don't let your expertise excuse your prayerlessness. You may be the smartest person in the room—but God still sees what you can't. He knows the terrain. The trapdoors. The timing…You don't.

So, when a door closes—don't kick it open. Ask why. Ask what God is protecting you from. Ask where He wants to lead you instead. Because that's what obedience looks like. Not blind action, but surrendered movement.

You don't have to know everything to follow God. You just have to trust that He does. And sometimes that trust looks like walking away from something that once looked like the perfect opportunity—but now feels like a quiet, "No."

And when it does? Let it go, because the outcome isn't the point. Obedience is.

Hindsight will tell you what happened. But only God can tell you what *will* happen. And He invites you to trust—not because He wants control, but because He *already* has the map.

Look to Jesus. If you're wondering whether you can trust God with your business, your decisions, your future—just look at His Son.

> *"The Son is the image of the invisible God,*
> *the firstborn over all creation."*
> — Colossians 1:15

This is why we don't just need more information. We need *revelation*. We don't need more credentials. We need *Christ*. We don't need another strategy session. We need a *Savior*.

So, the next time a door closes, pause. Don't push it back open.

Let God be the One who opens and shuts. Let Jesus be your wisdom. Let obedience be your legacy.

Because even the wisest among us can get it wrong—but God never does.

"And your ears shall hear a word behind you, saying, 'This is the way, walk in it,' when you turn to the right or when you turn to the left." - Isaiah 30:21 (ESV)

"Your business is what you do, but it's not who you are. Who you are is defined by whose you are."- Zig Zigler

"Commit your way to the Lord; trust in Him, and He will act." – Psalm 37:5

Chapter 15

What Comes Next?

So, you've gotten your feet wet, built a business, created a team, led with intention and with integrity. You have stopped when you should've stopped, and you're learning how to trust the voice of God in your business. Good job, but it's far from over. Maybe things have gone beautifully. Maybe your brand is on fire, or maybe it isn't. Once you're in for the long haul, when you've made the decision to keep moving, and fought every yearning to close your doors, the real work begins.

What comes next is rarely wrapped in clarity. More often, it comes in whispers. In questions. It's in the chaos of the challenges you didn't quite see coming and in the stressed-out smiles of your best employees.

But it's also in the quiet space after the door closes at night. After the final email is sent. After the last invoice is paid this month. You breathe. You exhale. You sit still—and somewhere inside, you whisper: Okay… now what?

People don't talk enough about what happens after the storm passes. After the pivot. After the risk. After the dream you fought for has unfolded in ways you thought it would or wouldn't. When you're left wondering what it all means now because next comes the real work. It's about choosing—intentionally, quietly, courageously— how you're going to build from here.

What comes next is undeniably unique for every business, every organization, every entrepreneur.

It could be a big win. It could be a six-figure launch or that magazine feature. A LinkedIn announcement or the applause of peers… or not.

Whether or not those things come, what always comes next is the Monday morning when you sit back down, coffee in hand, and start again—for the sixth or twentieth year in a row.

It's the way you decide to run your meetings—with compassion, with boundaries, with eyes that see the whole person behind the project. It's the conversation you have with a team member who's struggling, and how you choose to stay instead of retreat. It's the prayer you whisper before a tough decision–the moment you breathe through your anxiety and decide to respond with grace, not reactivity.

What comes next is rooted.

When I started this business, it wasn't for freedom or fame. It wasn't even for money—though, yes, we needed it. I started it because I wanted to provide. For my family. For my future. For a version of life where I wasn't apologizing for being who I am.

I wanted my child to see me build something honest. To watch faith in action. To witness what it looks like to work hard and love harder. But the truth is, I didn't understand the soil I was planting in back then. I didn't realize that the late nights, the heartbreaks, the grace-filled recoveries after hard conversations would be what shaped me.

And I surely didn't realize that everything I was learning—every email I rewrote, every "no" I wrestled with, every unseen tear I wiped at my desk—was preparing me for what's next.

I really do believe in full circles. So, at least for me, what comes next isn't about reinvention. It's about remembering.

I think often about my Nana's house, sitting quietly in the soybean fields of Northeast Arkansas. That place didn't just smell like home—it felt like foundation. A place where I didn't have to be strong or successful to be worthy of love. There were no speeches about legacy there. Just good food. Safe arms. A love that didn't ask you to earn it.

She worked hard, took in ironing, snapped beans, sewed for hours. She didn't post inspirational quotes. But her life was a lighthouse—anchored in faith, in kindness, in the belief that the people she loved mattered.

That's what I come back to when I ask, "What comes next?"

Because "next" isn't just about scale. It's not about getting louder. It's about going deeper. Becoming the good soil for someone else. Becoming the leader you once needed. The advocate you never had. The mentor who sees potential in someone who's still unsure they have any. What comes next is people.

I can list our services. I can point to the websites we've built, the campaigns we've launched, the awards we've won. But when I look at what comes next? It's this: A woman who didn't think she belonged in tech—and now she's leading a team. A client who came to us with shame in their voice—and now their voice is everywhere, because we helped them believe it deserved to be heard. A quiet creative who was told he wasn't strategic enough—and is now holding strategy meetings with confidence.

That's what we're building. That's what lasts for this lifetime and will influence generations beyond us all.

What comes next is faith on the ground: Matthew 5:16 says, "Let your light shine before others, that they may see your good deeds and glorify your Father in heaven." I used to think "light" meant charisma. Clarity. Answers.

Now I think light is what stays on when everything else goes dim. Light is the way you treat your team when things are tight. Light is the boundary you set, even though it might disappoint someone.

Light is the generosity that doesn't make it into your Instagram stories. Light is what you give, even when you feel like you're running out.

That's what I hope against hope I'm carrying into what's next. Not a legacy, per se—but a presence. A light. A willingness to let God's goodness echo through the work of my hands, the weight of my words, the integrity of my choices.

So, I'll ask you—not what legacy are you leaving…

But what are you building next? What rhythms are you rebuilding? What truth are you walking into? Who are you becoming, now that the last chapter has closed?

I hope you're answering this not with a resume, but with your heart:

"I'm building something real. Something kind. Something strong enough to weather storms and soft enough to hold others. I'm building what's next—with intention. With faith. With the God who's never left my side." Because what comes next won't be perfect, but it can be holy.

So go ahead, friend. Build. Do it on your terms and make it count.

Epilogue: Look for the Snowy Path

I want to leave you with one last story—maybe the most important piece of advice I have to give.

There was a time I found myself drawn to the slopes—not to ski (if you know me, you realize skiing would be my death), but to watch. There's something mesmerizing about it. There was a time I would sit with a thermos of coffee in hand, watching skiers carve their way down the mountainside, weaving through trees with this fearless grace. They dodge branches, slice through the forest, and every now and then, they take flight—launching off cliffs like they were born with wings, landing with a quiet precision that makes it look easy.

It blows my mind every time.

And I remember thinking: *How do they not hit the trees?* I mean, they're everywhere. Tall, unmoving, unforgiving.

So, I asked a friend who's an experienced skier. I expected a technical answer. Something about muscle memory or terrain reading. But instead, he just laughed and said, "Oh, that's easy. You don't look at the trees."

I blinked. "What do you mean? How else do you avoid them?"

He smiled. "If you look at the trees, you'll hit the trees. You've got to look at the snow. You've got to focus on the path."

That answer landed harder than I expected. I've carried it with me ever since.

Because here's the truth: life is a lot like that mountainside. The trees are real. The risks. The regrets. The moments that haunt us or make us hesitate. The distractions that pull us in a dozen directions. The fear that we'll fall or fail or not be enough. They stand tall, and they are everywhere.

But if we spend all our energy staring at what we want to avoid, we'll crash right into it.

If all you see is what might go wrong, you'll never move toward what could go right.

The only way through the forest is to keep your eyes on the snow—on the quiet, steady stretch of ground ahead. The path you've carved for yourself. The direction that calls you forward.

Focus there. Breathe there. Trust yourself there. That's how you build something that lasts. That's how you find your way out of the fear and into the life you were meant to live.

So whatever season you're in, whatever heartbreak or uncertainty or chaos you're navigating—don't let the trees steal your focus.

Look for the snow. Follow the path. And no matter what—keep going.

www.ingramcontent.com/pod-product-compliance
Lightning Source LLC
Chambersburg PA
CBHW071515140726
47997CB00005B/1980